People in Organisations

Title of related interest
R. S. Giles and J. W. Capel, *Finance and Accounting*

PEOPLE IN ORGANISATIONS

Edward Sallis
and
Kate Sallis

MACMILLAN
EDUCATION

First published 1988

Published by
MACMILLAN EDUCATION LTD
Houndmills, Basingstoke, Hampshire RG21 2XS
and London
Companies and representatives
throughout the world

Printed in Hong Kong

British Library Cataloguing in Publication Data
Sallis, Edward
   People in organisations.
   1. Organization
   I. Title   II. Sallis, Kate
   302.3'5'024658   HM131

   ISBN 0–333–43374–2

Contents

Acknowledgements   xi

Introduction   xii

SECTION I: STUDY   1

1 How to Study   3
Having a goal   3
Activity: 'What are your goals?'   4
Study — the preliminary steps   5
The diary method of learning   8
Making effective notes   8

2 Thinking and Creativity   12
Critical and creative thinking   13
Brainstorming   14
Key words   15

3 Managing your Time   17
Logging your time   18
Activity: 'A time log'   20
Negotiation on work schedules   20
Priorities and objectives   20

SECTION II: COMMUNICATION   23

4 What is Communication?   25
Analysing communication — the theory   25
Communication barriers   28
Oral communications   29
Qualities of speech   31
Listening   33
Improving listening skills   34

5 The Business Letter — **36**
What are business letters for? — 37
Corporate identity and logos — 37
Activity: 'Logos' — 38
Statutory requirements — 38
Other essential information and stationery style — 39
How to lay out a business letter — 40
Writing the letter — 46
Tone and style — 48
Standard letters and paragraphs — 49
Activity: 'Letter writing' — 49

6 The Memorandum — **51**
The format of the memo — 51
What are memos used for? — 53
Style — 53
Activity: 'Writing memos' — 54

7 Using the Telephone — **56**
Activity: 'Smiling voices' — 57
Receiving calls — 57
Making calls — 58

8 Report Writing — **60**
Types of report — 60
Writing a report — 61
Structure of reports — 63
Activity: 'Report writing' — 63

9 Press Releases — **64**
Writing a press release — 64
Activity: 'Designing a press release' — 66

10 Visual Presentation of Information — **67**
Thinking in pictures — 68
Varieties of presentation — 69
Bar charts — 69
Line graphs — 72
Combined bar and line graph — 75
Pie charts — 75
Bubble charts — 77
Activity: 'Bubble Charts Analysis' — 78
Pictograms — 78

11 Giving a Talk   **80**
Preparing for a talk   80
Activity: 'A talk'   82

12 Communicating by Computer   **84**
The language of computing   85
Some computer essentials   86
Activity: 'Word processing'   92
Electronic communications   93
Networking computers   94

13 Non-discriminatory Language   **98**
Activity: 'Alternative titles'   100

SECTION III: ORGANISATIONS   **103**

14 The Structure of Organisations   **105**
How are organisations structured?   106
Activity: 'An organisation chart'   107
Organisational design   107
Activity: 'College structure'   110
Response to technological change —
    mechanistic and organistic structures   110
Answers to 'organisation chart' activity   111
Formal and informal organisations   112

15 Organisational Concepts   **116**
Accountability   116
Activity: 'Accountability'   117
Authority   118
Activity: 'Sources of authority'   119
Bureaucracy   119
Delegation   120
Hierarchies   120
Management   122
Management style   123
Power   125
Responsibility   126
Span of control   127
Staff and line   127
Activity: 'College organisation chart'   128
Status   128
Answers to the 'sources of authority' activity   129

16 Meetings **130**
Types of meetings 131
Committee meetings 132
The 'hidden agenda' 134
Taking minutes 136
How to be successful at meetings 136

17 Information Systems **138**
Levels of information 139
Too much information 140
Why file? 140
Information sources 143
The impact of Information Technology 145

18 Management Services **147**
Methods of change 147
Managing by objectives 147
Organisation and Methods 149
The aims of Organisation and Methods 149
How O & M is carried out 150

19 Job Evaluation **154**
Why should some jobs be worth more than others? 154
Activity: 'Job evaluation' 155
Methods of job evaluation 157
Job ranking 158
Activity: 'Job ranking' 158
Paired comparisons 159
Analytical methods 159
Job evaluation procedure under points rating 161
Criticisms of job evaluation 162

SECTION IV: PEOPLE **165**

20 Groups **167**
What is a group? 167
Activity: 'Group membership' 168
Formal and informal groups 169
What are groups good at? 169
Group norms 170
Stages of group development 171
Features of an effective work group 172
Behaviour in groups 173
Group roles 174
Interactions in groups 175

Quality circles 177
Activity: 'Analysing a work group' 178

21 Self-presentation **180**
Roles 181
How should I put my message across? 182
Yourself and others 183
Being assertive 185
Structuring arguments and persuading others 186

22 Motivation and Human Needs **190**
What is motivation? 191
Human needs 191
Activity: 'Motivation — a self-analysis' 191
Personnel policy and human needs 193
Is money a motivator? 195
The hygiene/motivator theory 196
What should an interesting job contain? 197
Activity: 'Your own motivation' 198
Equity theory 198
Activity: 'Equity and motivation' 199
Expectations and motivation 199
Job satisfaction 200

23 The Employment Process **202**
The selection process — the employer's needs 202
Employee specification 203
Activity: 'Describe yourself — a self-appraisal exercise' 203
Human resource planning 204
Where do I look for a job? 208
Application forms and CVs 210
Activity: 'Analysis of Sheila's CV' 213
Activity: 'Letter of application' 218
Preparing for an interview 218
Types of interviews 220
Interview questions 223

24 Performance Appraisal **226**
Does every organisation have a form of staff appraisal? 226
The purpose of appraisal 227
Appraisal methods 229
Self-appraisal 231
An appraisal interview checklist 231
Activity: 'Preparing for the annual appraisal interview' 233

25 Opportunities and Change   **234**
     What business am I in?   234
     Activity: 'Opportunities'   236
     The problem of change   236
     How to recognise opportunities   237
     SWOTs   237
     Activity: 'New ideas'   239
     Career planning   239
     Activity: 'Career planning'   241

SECTION V: ASSIGNMENTS   **243**

1   Mapping the College's Structure   245
2   The Press Release   246
3   Applying for a Job   249
4   Facing up to Change   252
5   Systems Analysis   254

Bibliography   257

Index   259

Acknowledgements

The Training Office at Guildford College of Technology performed sterling work in typing the manuscript and coping with our near illegible handwriting. The students and the Training Office Manager, Joy Bell, deserve our thanks. Without them there would be no book.

We could never have written this book without the help of the countless students we have taught over the years and who have provided the stimulus for our thinking. The experience of working in BTEC teams at Somerset College of Arts and Technology provided the initial motivation, and team teaching with Joyce Miles the inspiration for writing the book. Our colleagues at Guildford College of Technology, East Surrey College and Bracknell College have been a tremendous source of help and ideas. To all our colleagues past and present go our thanks.

Extracts from BS 3138: 1979 are reproduced by permission of BSI. Complete copies can be obtained from them at Linford Wood, Milton Keynes, MK14 6LE.

The quoted material on pages 162–163 is reproduced with the permission of the *Times Educational Supplement*.

Guildford, 1987   Edward and Kate Sallis

Introduction

Work is carried out by people in organisations. Hence the title of the new BTEC Unit for the National Level courses in Business and Finance, Distribution Studies, Public Administration, and Leisure Studies. 'People in Organisations' is also the theme as well as the title of this book. Its aim is to assist you explore the major activities which people do and which affect them at work. Examples of the type of questions which the book seeks to answer are;

'What makes us work?'
'What use can we make of information technology and how does it affect our working lives?'
'What exactly is a job and how is it best designed?'
'How can we make ourselves better at seeking jobs and planning our careers?'
'How is work best organised?'
'How can our success be measured?'
'How can we make ourselves better communicators?'
'How can we become more effective at work?'
'Are we sufficiently aware of the needs of others?'

In short, this book aims to help you to become a more effective member of an organisation. It is not all you will need. Your lecturers' notes and directions and the assignments you are given to perform are important complementary activities to those in this book. No textbook can do justice to every aspect of a syllabus. In this book we have sought to cover the important aspects of human resources in organisations as they affect students studying for BTEC awards, but we make no claims to be comprehensive in our coverage. The book is one of the many aids to learning and only a part of your total educational experience.

All of you have some experience of organisations to which you can relate. Those of you in employment or on Youth Training Schemes have your companies, while full-time students have their colleges and their work

experience placements. Most of you are also members of other organisations and these can be useful when you need to make comparisons. Many
of you are members of clubs, societies, and other organisations such as
voluntary bodies and trade unions. In addition, during your course you will
visit offices and factories and, of course, go shopping. Shopping and leisure
visits to places like swimming pools, museums, concert halls, theatres and
sports centres can provide interesting insights into how organisations work.
How often have you been into a shop and said "this place is inefficient", or
"this is my favourite shop — the assistants are always knowledgeable and
friendly", or again "they really ought to improve the layout here, one
cannot find anything." All of these are organisational judgements. What
most of us usually do is to stop there and rarely ask why a particular place
works well or gives a good service and another does not. If you are to build
up your knowledge, you are going to require a framework to help you
analyse how organisations operate.

You also need to know how organisations communicate with their
customers and clients. You need to be interested in what sort of people
they employ. In order for an organisation to function well a large number
of complex factors come into play: finance, marketing, technology,
competition, human resources, and it is the interplay of these forces that a
BTEC course is about.

In addition, this book is concerned with *PEOPLE* and in particular
YOU. It is a well-worn cliché that an organisation is only as good as the
people working in it, but it is nevertheless true. You will want to know how
best to prepare yourself for working life, how to relate to others, and to
discover what an organisation expects of you.

The authors have taught BTEC students at First, National, Higher
National and Continuing Education levels, and as a result we know the
demanding yet fascinating time which BTEC students can have on their
course. We are committed to a student-centred approach to learning and
we believe that you learn best by taking part in activities.

In order to promote this approach we have included a number of
activities in this book. They are designed to help you develop your skills.
They are not full-blown assignments although many could be readily
adapted. We appreciate that most lecturers and course teams prefer to
write their own material and rarely use many of the assignments provided
in textbooks. The majority of the activities in this book have been designed
for individual students to carry out in their own time to supplement
assignment work. The exercises are designed to provide the impetus for
deeper thought about the topic in question. A small number of full-scale
assignments are included in Section V.

SECTION I

STUDY

CHAPTER 1

How to Study

One of the most useful skills you can learn, and one that will be of benefit throughout your life, is how to study. Studying documents, procedures, reports, plans and other working papers will be a part of your life well after you have finished your BTEC course.

In order to study effectively you need to be organised and to put sufficient time aside to learn and to reflect. The aim of your study is for you to *LEARN*. This we define as the process of acquiring new knowledge and skills, and critically assessing the views and attitudes which you hold.

> *You learn best if you have a clear idea of why you are learning something. It is important to have a goal at which to aim when you are studying.*

Having a goal

In order to study effectively you need to start by being certain in your own mind what it is you are studying, and what it is you want to learn. In order to go down this path you need a *GOAL* — something to aim at which will make all the study and learning worthwhile. Unless you have a goal your learning will be an uphill struggle. Of course, some people are very lucky and always know exactly why they are doing things. With planning it is possible for all of us to clarify our thoughts about our hopes and future needs.

In order to start the process of formulating goals you need to ask yourself some fundamental questions about your own motivation. The activity which follows is designed to assist you in doing this.

Activity: 'What are your goals?'

You should do this exercise as honestly as possible. There are no right answers. It is useful to carry out this exercise in pairs. One person should ask the other the questions and record the answers, and then the process is reversed. You should discuss the implications of your answers with your partner at the end of the exercise.

'Are you interested in money?'
'Are you concerned about status?'
'Is your main goal happiness?'
'Are friends important to you?'
'Is your social life important to you?'
'What interests and hobbies would you give up for advancement at work?'
'Would you be prepared to move home for work?'
'Would you be prepared to take an interesting job at a low salary?'
'What do you want out of life?'
'What is it about work that gives you the most pleasure?'
'What is it that you dislike most about work?'
'What are your career ambitions?'
'How have you planned to make a success of your career?'
'Do you intend to carry on studying after you have completed this course?'
'Do you find study difficult?'
'What are the main barriers you find to studying?'
'How have you planned to make your study more effective?'

Only you can answer questions about your motivation. There are various activities in this book to help you know yourself better. The importance of these is that they make you think and help you recognise what it is that 'makes you tick'. Once you know this, you can establish a goal or a series of goals which will then give you a purpose for your studies. When the going gets tough with your studies, having goals will help to see you through.

Study — the preliminary steps

Be clear in your own mind what is involved in the course which you are studying. This is particularly true of the BTEC National which has a complex course structure. Your course will have started with an

A Goal for Karen

Karen had always wanted to travel and see the world. Yet she realised that she also had a strong need for security. She did well at subjects like geography and foreign languages at school which reflected her interests in other countries and cultures.

Karen realised that her goal was to find a job which was challenging and interesting and which provided her with opportunities for foreign travel.

Once she had identified her goals she, together with her BTEC Course Tutor at her College, chose options on the National Diploma which allowed her to pursue these aims. She studied, among other option units, Travel and Tourism, Economic Geography and French.

Karen made application early in the second year of the course to a number of major national travel companies as an overseas representative. She undertook work experience with a tour operator to find out whether the reality matched her expectations. She found that establishing her own goals based on her needs made studying that much easier and gave a purpose to the activities and assignments she was asked to do on the course. Karen found a job with a major travel company after she completed her course. The study skills she had learnt were certainly of value — six weeks before she went on her first overseas assignment her company put her through a crash course in Greek!

induction period when some of the demands of the course will have been explained to you. You need to make clear notes about what is being expected of you. In particular, you need to be certain about how many assignments you will be given and when you are expected to hand them in.

A good idea, used by many students, is to draw up a grid showing the weeks the assignments are handed out, the hand-in dates and the grades you have achieved. It is useful to put this information on the inside cover of a loose-leaf course folder. If you do this exercise it will provide you with an idea of how much time to spend on each assignment. Examples of how you might do this are shown in figures 1 and 2.

Find a suitable place to study where you feel happy and comfortable. This may be difficult at home but you will work better if you have a desk in a room where you can do uninterrupted work. Some people work better to music while others do not. If you find music helps your concentration then use it. Pay attention to the level of lighting and never sit in the shadow. If you develop eye strain it might be because you are reading too close to the

Unit / Week	People in organisations Assignment No.	Grade	Organisation in its environment Assignment No.	Grade	Finance Assignment No.	Grade	Information processing Assignment No.	Grade
1	1							
2							1	
3	Hand in	Dist.	1					
4					1		Hand in	Merit
5			Hand in	Merit				
6	2							
7					Hand in	Pass	2	
etc.								

Figure 1   Assignment schedule

printed page. About eighteen inches is the optimum distance between eye and page.

Set yourself a personal timetable for study. It is quite unrealistic to think that you can spend every waking moment working, but it is equally unrealistic to have hobbies and interests which fill every evening and the weekend and for you to expect to pass the course.

Study takes time and the best way to use it is to set yourself a programme. *REGULAR STUDY* is the most successful way to learn. It is a good idea to put aside two evenings a week and, say, a Sunday afternoon on a regular basis.

Times for study are important but personal things. Through trial and error you need to establish what times suit you best and then keep to them. Some people study best for a couple of hours straight after coming home from work or college. Others work better late at night, while a few people

Assignments / Units	1	2	3	4	5	Overall Grade
People in organisations	Dist.	Merit	Merit	Dist.	Dist.	Distinction
Organisation in its environment	Pass	Merit	Pass	Merit	Merit	Merit
Finance	Merit	Dist.	Merit	Merit	Dist.	Merit
Information Processing	Pass	Pass	Merit	Merit	Dist.	Merit

Figure 2   Analysis — grades in year 1

prefer to be up early in the morning and study before they go to work. Regardless of your preference you should try to establish a pattern.

Do not work for long periods without a break. Long periods of continuous study are very tiring. An effective period of study is about twenty to twenty-five minutes. Try breaking a period of study into twenty minute blocks. You should make a cup of tea in one break, take a short walk around the block in another. In this way you will return refreshed to your study.

An important study aid is to keep an indexed set of files. It is important to file away your classwork notes carefully so that you are able to find them again when you need them. Some people find it helpful to write out their notes again before they file them. They find that the act of repetition helps the learning process.

Do keep your notes in good order. Loose-leaf binders are the most flexible means of keeping notes and hand-outs tidy. You can use coloured dividers to classify them into subjects.

Above all, enjoy your study. If you think of it as fun then it will become a pleasure. Achievement is one of the most important means of finding satisfaction. If you have developed the skills for effective study from your course, then you will have achieved a great deal.

The diary method of learning

Your course and this book can provide you with activities and ideas to guide your study, but it is you who have to do the learning.

One useful way of assisting your learning is to keep a diary. A diary helps you to reflect and it aids memory. You can learn both from your successes and mistakes.

Keeping a diary is a time-consuming activity but you can keep it within manageable bounds by being selective in the events you record. A good place to start is to record the experiences you have in group activities. These experiences can be rewarding, frustrating, elating and even painful, but they are usually memorable. You may decide to ponder on why sometimes you are the centre of attention and why at others you are an outsider, or how alliances are formed, or why a group works well in one situation and becomes bogged down in other circumstances?

The idea we are putting to you is to keep a diary of certain of the major aspects of the course and to use it as an aid to reflection and learning.

Making effective notes

There is an activity which will take a great deal of your time as a student, which is of crucial importance to your success and which passes with hardly a mention on many courses — we refer, of course, to note-taking. Everyone assumes that students know how to make and use their notes, and yet time and time again a piece of work does not receive the grade it deserves because crucial material or ideas have been left out; often this is information which the lecturer gave out in classes but which the student did not note down. Making good notes in lectures or from books is an important art and a useful skill. It will stand you in good stead throughout your life because effective note-taking is as important in business as it is to study.

Why make notes?

Notes are important for the following reasons:

- Note-taking aids concentration when you are listening to a lecture, watching a video or reading a book or article. If you do not make notes your mind will have a tendency to wander and you will quickly lose the thread of the ideas with which you are trying to come to terms. Making notes is the best way of keeping your mind on the task at hand.

- Note-taking provides a means of ordering your thoughts and ideas about any particular subject.
- Note-taking provides references which are essential for assignment and examination preparation. Most people's long-term memory is very limited when it comes to remembering specific points or ideas. Of course, you can always refer to books but this is rarely convenient if you have a piece of work to do for a deadline. Your own notes are personal to you and ordered by you so that it is relatively easy to find the material you want when you want it. Without a good set of notes you will handicap yourself when it comes to assignment and examination preparation.
- Note-taking helps you think, select and remember. It provides your work with *organisation* which is the key to understanding. The ability to remember information is related directly to the importance which it has for you. The more time you have spent making notes from lectures or from books and rewriting and ordering those notes, the greater the importance that material will be to you. You will have invested time and effort in the activity and you have a vested interest in seeing a return from the investment.

How to make notes

There is a range of different types of note-taking and each has its place. You should select and practise the appropriate method for the task in hand.

Verbatim notes are used where you want to record everything that is being said in a lecture or copy exactly what appears in print in a book or magazine article. You will only want to do this on rare occasions. Unless you are a shorthand writer you will not have the speed to make verbatim notes from a talk and there is rarely the need to copy out material from books. The photocopier will do the latter job for you. Verbatim notes provide an exact record of what has been said or what happened, but the times when you require this are extremely limited. It is the process of paraphrasing, ordering and abbreviating which helps to fix material in the memory.

Sequential notes follow the pattern as laid down by the lecturer or speaker, or record the pattern of thought of the author whose book you are making notes from. In order to summarise a lecture you need to *listen* carefully to the lecturer and record the main points as they are made. The best way to do this is to have a series of numbered points with headings and then to write concise summaries under each heading. It is useful to jot down a few examples under each point as this aids understanding and memory.

DO NOT WORRY ABOUT WRITING IN COMPLETE SEN-TENCES. Most students invent their own shorthand and shortforms. The important thing about notes is that you understand them. You should write your notes up in continuous prose as soon as possible after the lecture so that you do not forget what the shortforms stand for. This also has the advantage of allowing you to add material which you have remembered but have not written down.

When taking notes it is important to write down any new words or concepts, even if you do not understand them at the time. You should research them as you write up your notes and prepare precise definitions which can be referred to later.

Classified and patterned notes follow the pattern determined by the student and not by the lecturer. Individuals find their own style of creative note-taking. Some people use a series of boxes, while others start with the lecture title in a centre circle with the main points radiating from it. Arrows and lines are used to link related points. In this form of note-taking, only keywords and main points are recorded, and it is important to copy up the notes soon after the lecture in order to fix the train of thought. The advantage of the method is it blends creativity with listening.

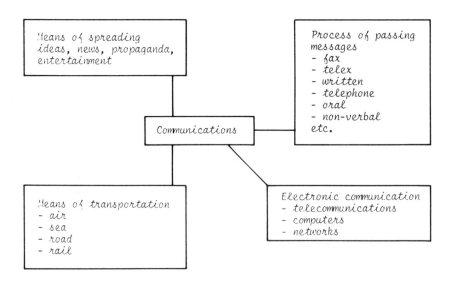

Asking questions

Up until now we have given the impression that note-taking is a fairly passive activity, albeit one that can be creative. In order to gain as much as possible from a lecture or reading a book, it is important to ask questions in order to answer queries as they arise. This is easy to do in lectures. You should jot questions down as they occur to you during the talk. Some of them will be answered in the lecture but those that are not should be asked at an appropriate point. Asking questions and preparing to ask questions is an important part of note-taking. It makes you think about what you are listening to and it gives you an active role in the lecture process. Similarly, points which occur to you when you are reading should be brought up either in class or in a tutorial with your lecturer. A positive approach to study of this nature makes it more interesting and provides a degree of excitement.

Thinking and Creativity

A major aspect of any course of study is the development of your powers of reasoning and thinking. One of the main set of attributes looked for by employers in their recruits is their ability to find interesting, creative and workable solutions to problems.

> *There are many people who are scared of thinking as an activity. They believe that creative thought is only for clever people. This is not the case. Thinking is a skill and like any other it can be developed and improved through practice.*

Before we discuss how you can develop your creative powers, we need to make a distinction between two different but related activities — *THINKING* and *LEARNING*.

Traditional academic courses stress *learning*. If you take a degree in English Literature or International Relations, you will do so with the intention of *learning* about the subject. That is to say, your study will provide you with the knowledge that is generally accepted as making up the subject. This is true to some extent on a Business Studies course, but learning about commercial activity is only a part of your studies. What is different about a vocational course is that you are also expected to be creative and to produce new ideas, novel applications and improved methods of doing things. In short, you will be required to apply the principles of *thinking* on a regular and systematic basis.

Of course, thinking and learning are necessarily intertwined. Thinking requires prior knowledge and learning — it makes little sense to reinvent the wheel — but too much emphasis on learning what has been the case can inhibit the growth of thinking about how to do things in unusual and interesting ways.

Business courses place an importance on creative thought because it is new ideas which keep a business ahead of its competition. Often problems seem intractable because the same solutions are tried time and time again without success, whereas what is needed is a new approach and fresh thinking.

Critical and creative thinking

There are two main forms of thinking — *critical* and *creative*. Both are powerful in their own way, but each has a different purpose and a different end. Academic study has tended to emphasise critical thought as the natural companion to learning a subject. Students are often asked to criticise such and such an author's views, or to appraise critically the outcome of a particular idea or thought. It is important to subject views, ideas and actions to thorough examination. It exposes flaws and loopholes; and, by analysis, contradictions are highlighted and the limitations of proposals are exposed. As a method of thought it is important as it helps to prevent bad ideas or decisions from being implemented.

The purpose of critical appraisal is to show up the effects of a proposal before time and effort are invested in putting an idea into action.

> *Creative thinking is the process of developing new ideas, new inventions and novel ways of doing things. It often involves looking at problems afresh and giving serious consideration to ideas which have traditionally been regarded as impossible or impracticable.*

Critical thinking is, however, essentially negative as it seeks to dissect and not to build. Creative thinking is different and it is the process of dreaming up new schemes and finding solutions to problems. A good illustration of the difference between the two types of thought is given by the two National Diploma students who had analysed what they wanted from a job when they had finished at college. They came up with a vision of work that offered them a challenge, was interesting and in which they were in charge. Many of their friends were *critical*. They did not think that these qualities could be found in a job for college leavers — "Well perhaps interest and challenge, but not being in charge." For the two students some *creative* thinking provided the solution — to set up in business of their own.

Many people shy away from creative thinking. Its application does put its exponents in the firing line of critical appraisal. There are those who feel uncomfortable with the exposure critical thinking brings. It does, however, have its consolations because developing new ideas can be a stimulating and exciting experience, especially if they come to fruition.

There is another reason for the reluctance to indulge in creative thinking and that is because it is often confused with original thought. The very idea of coming up with something so novel that no one has thought of it is daunting. The truth is that most creative thinking is not of this magnitude. Instead it involves such things as finding new uses for old products or showing how solutions considered impracticable can be made to work.

There are organisations which take a positive approach to creative thinking and build it into their staff development structure by organising creative days or even weeks. During these, competitions may be held for ideas which will improve the efficiency and effectiveness of the organisation. Every employee is encouraged to produce ideas and no suggestion, however small, is rejected without serious consideration. Sections and departments hold brainstorming sessions and posters are displayed to encourage the climate of innovation. The purpose is to create a permanent creative thinking culture in which all employees, regardless of grade and status, come to regard thinking as an essential element of their role.

Brainstorming

The Secretarial Section of a Business Studies Department was concerned about the rising cost of the paper which the students used during their typewriting practice. Ideas were sought to find a solution. The thought which came most readily was to restrict the amount of paper which each student could use and to force them to be more economical with it. However, this was seen as a rather negative solution to the problem and so another more positive approach was tried — *brainstorming*. Staff and students sat down together to engage in an exercise in creative thought. The rules were simple — do not analyse the problem, just devise solutions. All ideas, however unusual, would be considered. Fifteen minutes were put aside for this activity and over twenty-five suggestions were recorded, although some were overlapping. Here is a selection:

"Charge all students a small sum of money each year to cover the paper they use."
"Put all the waste paper through a shredder and sell it in the college shop as bedding for rabbits and guinea pigs."
"Find a sponsor for the Secretarial Section — perhaps a local employment agency or a paper manufacturer."
"Reorganise the practice office so that the students do 'live work' instead of assignments. A charge could be made for the work carried out and this could offset the cost of the paper."
"Form a parent/student association to organise social and fund-raising activities."
"Cease purchasing typewriters and in future buy word processors so that most corrections can be done on the screen."

This example shows what can be done by brainstorming. The purpose is to be creative. No idea is ruled out during the period of the brainstorming.

A brainstorming session is devoted to creative thought. Generally speaking, as brainstorming sessions get underway the ideas start to flow and one person's good idea stimulates another person's thoughts. What often starts as a trickle finishes up as a torrent of new ideas. Ten or fifteen minutes is usually long enough for the activity. It is only at the end of a session when creativity is exhausted that the results are subjected to criticism and appraisal and an attempt is made to analyse what has been suggested. It helps to carry out this activity in a group but individuals can use the method with equal success.

> *The idea of a brainstorming session is to look forward. All ideas, however absurd, should be expressed.*

A variant on this approach is *lateral thinking*, made famous by Edward de Bono. This involves making random leaps and jumps in thinking in order to develop novel ways of problem solving. Logic and precision are put aside and the final solution is more important than the steps which lead to it. The basis of lateral thinking is to be provocative with your ideas and to put them forward however bizarre or ridiculous they sound on first hearing. The idea that supermarkets should be built on green field sites out of town rather than in the High Street would have seemed absurd only a few years ago.

Key words

A useful way of developing creative thinking and one which can be of great benefit when you are studying and looking for inspiration is the technique of *key words* or *key terms*. This technique is also known as *word association* or the *association of ideas*. The idea is simply to take the subject or problem with which you are dealing and write it in the centre of a piece of blank paper.

The next stage is to jot down every idea or word which comes into your mind which you associate with it. It is, of course, only brainstorming by another name but, by creating the planetary diagrams which are a fundamental part of the technique, you find that certain patterns of thought start to emerge. You may, for example, have been given an assignment to do on the organisation of a business. When you look at it you realise that organisation can mean a variety of things — which is the one that you are expected to write about? This is where the key word technique can be of value. Write the word organisation in the centre of a blank sheet of paper and map everything that you associate with it which comes into your mind. As with brainstorming, do not reject anything at this stage. It is only after you have the key words on paper that you can begin to structure them.

This idea is of great benefit in examinations. Many students find it useful to spend two or three minutes drawing a key words map for the questions they intend to answer. The very act of brainstorming often throws up the structure of the answer as well as the main points which it is necessary to cover.

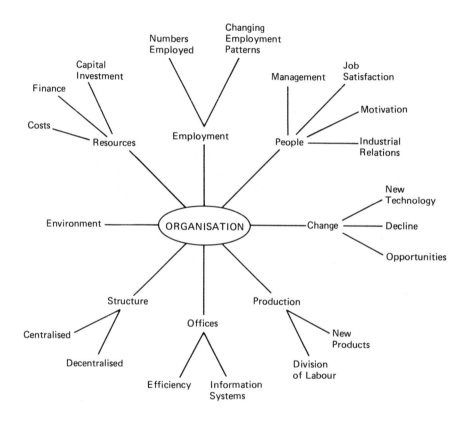

CHAPTER 3

Managing your Time

In order to make a success of study, you need to learn how to manage your time. The plain fact is that time is limited. Take out of a typical day the classes you must attend, the time spent travelling, the hours you sleep, the eating, shopping, meeting friends, relaxing, watching television, listening to music and all the other activities of a busy day, and there is not much time left for study.

Students and business people alike are faced with the challenge of making the best use of their time. You should think of time as a resource and, like any resource, it can be squandered or utilised in an effective and efficient manner. We are certain that you will be aware of how some people are able to achieve more than others, cram so much more into a working day, and do it with seemingly little effort. Those who have this skill are usually no brighter or cleverer than others but they do have an element in their make up which others lack — they are organised.

> The key to successful time management is knowing what you want to achieve, how much it means to you, and how much of your time and energy you are prepared to devote to it.

Successful time management allows you to do more than merely cope with your study or your work in the office. It can provide you with time itself. One essential ingredient of organising your work is to be able to put aside enough time in the day for thought and reflection. This is both a luxury and a necessity. It is a necessity because it provides the opportunity for reflection on how well you have carried out various tasks and whether there are better ways of doing things. It allows you to check that you have not forgotten to do essential jobs and, if you have, it provides the chance to rectify the mistake. But good time management also gives the luxury for future planning. Looking forward is a theme in many areas of this book. Life is more interesting if you are able to guide your own destiny, and this is only possible if you can find the time to plan.

Logging your time

Many people operate in a haphazard way. They give little thought to what they have to do in a day and how long each task may take. They do not set themselves objectives to achieve. In consequence they are often disappointed with how they have spent their time or with what they have achieved. If you are in this category and want to get out of it, or if you want to improve your organisation, then keeping a *time log* is a good place to start. It is very easy to do. It consists of a record of all the things you do in a day and, in order for it to be of value, you need to log every activity you are engaged in for at least one week, if not for two.

TIME LOG

DAY: TUESDAY   DATE: 17th FEBRUARY

Time	Activity	Place	Comment
0730			
0800	Get up/bathe	Home	Could get up earlier
0830	Breakfast	Home	
0900	Travel to College	Travel	Too much of a rush
0930	O&E Lecture	College	
1000		Room 106	Compulsory
1030			attendance
1100			
1130	Coffee	Canteen	I wasted some
1200			time here
1230	Lunch	Canteen	
1300			
1330			
1400	People in Organisations	Room 107	Compulsory
1430	Lecture		attendance
1500			
1530			
1600	Study in the library	Library	Unproductive — I
1630			forget the key book
1700			
1730	Travel home	Travel	
1800	Arrive home. Did not do		Unproductive
1830	very much before		
	supper	Home	
1900	Supper		
1930			

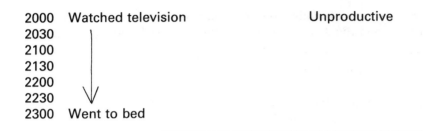

2000	Watched television	Unproductive
2030		
2100		
2130		
2200		
2230		
2300	Went to bed	

Analysis of activities	Total time spent on each	Comment
Eating/dressing/bathing	4	Could be reduced
Lectures	4	Could make better notes during these
Travel	1	Cannot be reduced
Library study	$1\frac{1}{2}$	Not well used
Loafing around	$1\frac{1}{2}$	Relaxation is necessary
Television	3	Much of this was a waste of time

Overall comments
Not a very productive day. I could find at least three hours here for study and reflection. I will try to do this tomorrow.

The very activity of keeping a log focuses attention on how you have used your time. You need to be honest with yourself and ask whether your time has been used profitably. Do not be concerned that a part of your day is given up to relaxation and leisure. These are necessary and you cannot spend all of your time studying. What you need to do is to decide how much time study requires and then find the time in the day to do it.

Some people are dismayed when they first start to keep a log. If this happens to you, do not be concerned. Most people could make better use of their time and the whole idea of the log is to provide the information and stimulus for improvement. The important thing is to be happy with what you are doing with your life. If you are content with what you do then this is all that matters. If, on the other hand, you are not, then you need to make the effort and change the priority you give to the organisation of time.

Keeping a log and a study diary (described in the previous chapter) are useful disciplines. People who keep regular diaries find that the records become a source of motivation. You start to see a pattern developing in your study and you do not want to let yourself down by not studying today.

Activity: 'A time log'

Keep a detailed log of your activities during the next two weeks. You will need to be disciplined and honest in keeping it. At the end of the fortnight, write an *Action Plan* for the way you intend to use your time during the next two weeks. You should continue to keep the time log to see whether the actual use of time conforms to the goals you set in the Action Plan.

Negotiation on work schedules

At the start of your course you will be provided with a schedule informing you how many assignments you will be expected to do, with the dates for them to be handed out and collected in. In the previous section we suggested that you devise a simple diary to log in these assignments. If you do this you are unlikely to face the problem of forgetting about work and having inadequate time to do an assignment justice. Nevertheless, one problem which faces all students is that however well they plan, they may still fall behind with their work. It is not always their fault. Illness or a domestic problem can be the cause.

If this happens to you, do not panic. Worry causes stress, and this in turn can make the problem worse. You need restful sleep for any study and this does not happen if you are suffering from stress. Many students do not realise that they can negotiate alterations to assignment deadlines if they run into difficulties. If you are behind we recommend you do this. It is an important aspect of proper time management. If you realise that you cannot make the schedule, then you need to negotiate a realistic alternative. But remember that you will be under pressure after the negotiation, as the work has to be completed. It is at this point that proper forward planning and the use of the time log become of crucial importance.

Priorities and objectives

Forward planning consists simply of working out what you have to do to make a success of your course, working out how much time you require to complete the tasks and then breaking those tasks down into weekly schedules. Within each schedule you need to identify the priorities and to make certain that you give them their due weight and tackle them first. All of us have a tendency to put off the difficult tasks or those we dislike. You will need to be honest with yourself when setting priorities because on occasions the most important tasks may be the ones you feel least disposed towards.

It is important to put the plan in writing. The very act of writing it out clarifies what you need to do and provides you with an agenda to work towards. You should use the plan as a checklist for your future activities and as a monitoring document to show you how you performed against the plan.

SECTION II

COMMUNICATION

What is Communication?

Communication has a number of different but related meanings:

- Communication is the process of passing messages — ideas, information, beliefs — from one person to another person(s). This can take a multiplicity of forms including signals, gestures, speech, letters, telex, telephone, morse code, fax, television and radio.
- Communication is the name given to transport and travel facilities which enable people and goods to move from one place to another. We talk about 'channels of communication' when we discuss air travel or the proposed fixed rail link being constructed under the English Channel. It includes road, rail, air and sea transport. Communication in this sense is not a topic of discussion in this book, although it will form an element of your course in the Organisation in its Environment unit.
- Communication is a means of spreading news, ideas, propaganda, advertising and entertainment to large, often multi-national, audiences. The mass media embrace newspapers, books, magazines, radio, television, theatre, video and film.
- Communication of data via computerised and electronic means is a relatively new mode of communications but one which in the space of about thirty years has revolutionised the way in which we use, store and transmit information and data. It has opened up, via satellite and telecommunication links, sophisticated means of communication for a vast range of purposes including the control of spacecraft, weather forecasting and news transmission, and has provided us with vast and easily accessible data banks.

Analysing communication — the theory

How do we communicate? What is the process and what happens when people give and exchange messages?

The communication process

The mechanics of communications are:

sender — transmitter
signal   — code
channel — receiver

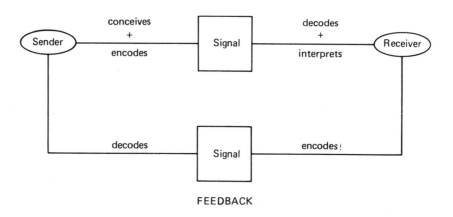

FEEDBACK

Let us consider a simple situation. A person (the message sender) enters a room and sees another person he or she recognises, and decides to send a recognition signal to them.

The message or signal has to be 'encoded'. The sender has a choice of means. The message could be spoken — "hello Jill" — or a non-verbal media could be employed — a wave. It is conceivable that the sender could set up a board and easel and compose a poem to signal to another, or write a message on a piece of paper and make a paper aeroplane to fly across the room. But, of course, many of our means of communication are instinctive and we have practised them so frequently since childhood that we choose the means of encoding a message almost without thought. This is the case with our recognition example. On other occasions the encoding process might be the result of a great deal of consideration. We often have to decide 'shall I write or would it be better to explain the matter in person . . . ?

The important part of the communication process is to encode the message in such a way that the receiver *understands* the message and the meaning behind it. It is important that we achieve our objective because misunderstandings may lead to embarrassment, hurt, anger or rejection. Many modes of communication may serve the purpose but we will need to choose one which is personally and socially acceptable, and does not provoke anger, surprise, or obscure the message. We might enter the room and sing our greeting accompanied by a few dance steps, but ask yourself whether the message might not be obliterated by the way our actions would be interpreted.

The signal has to be seen as one which is appropriate for putting our message across. Let us assume that in the split second that it took our sender to walk into the room and to recognise another person, a decision was made to smile. The smile is then a signal of recognition.

The process of communication does not end here. You have probably experienced smiling at someone you know closely followed by embarrassment, surprise and rejection when they did not recognise you, and instead of receiving the expected smile in return you were met by a blank stare. Your signal has to be decoded and understood by the receiver. The smile has to be *understood* by the other person as what it was meant to be — a friendly greeting.

It is at this point that things often go wrong and *communication breakdowns* occur. Other people cannot act on your message unless they have understood it. The problem is that understanding is a personal process and depends on so many different factors. We decode messages in personal, social and cultural contexts. If a person walks into a room and says "bonjour", our decoding process and actions will depend on whether we understand sufficient French to decode the message successfully and reply appropriately.

Very many misunderstandings occur because messages are decoded in ways in which they were not intended to be. We have to be aware of this possibility and, if we find that we are being misunderstood, find another means of expressing ourselves. If our smile does not receive a response we may try a more straightforward communication — "hello Jill, it's good to see you again."

Once the receiver has decoded the message and interpreted it, they must then decide how to act upon it. Once the smile has been interpreted as a greeting, the receiver has to decide on an appropriate means of *feedback*. The process of feedback follows the same pattern of encoding, signalling and decoding.

The art of communication is to know how your message is being received by others and how to respond to the messages you receive.

From this discussion the following conclusions can be drawn about the nature of communications:

- Communication is a *two way process*. It requires a sender and a receiver.
- Appropriate signals have to be employed if a message is to be understood.
- Even in simple communication there is plenty of room for error, ambiguity and uncertainty. For this reason you have to be aware of the effect which your communication has on other people.
- If you have not been understood, you have not communicated.

Communication barriers

A popular phrase is 'know what I mean?' Perhaps the reason why so many people say it or use the other favourite, 'you know', at the end of sentences is that they are uncertain whether other people understand them. "I am always misunderstood" is another common cry for help. If people do not understand you, is it their fault or yours? Why is the message not reaching its audience and can you do anything to change things so that it does? The answer to the first part of the question is that communication problems can be caused both by the sender and the receiver, but if you are frequently misinterpreted you may need to think about the message and the manner in which it is being transmitted.

Barriers to communications are common and they cause misunderstanding, frustration, hurt and anger. There are people who blame most of the problems in human affairs on communication failures, and they have a point. It may be an over-simplification, but imagine the improvement to our daily lives if everyone always understood everyone else, and if our speech and actions were always interpreted in the way we intended.

Listed below are some of the more common communication blocks and barriers:

- *The receiver is not listening.* This is one of the most common reasons for communication failure. We are often so anxious to talk, to express our views or to make our point, that we often fail to *listen* to what is being said to us. If we return to the theory we started with, we will realise that we have not even bothered to decode the message. Listening is an important skill and one we all need to develop. Being a good listener is not only useful because you will hear what others miss, but you will find that people will tell you things that they shield from others. (For a further discussion on listening see pages 33 to 35.)

- *The sender and the receiver are speaking different languages.* This may be the case literally when a French speaker has to communicate with a non-French speaker but, even within a common language, usage varies enormously. Accent, tone, fluency and vocabulary can affect the ability of sender and receiver to understand or to be understood. We are all aware of the problems of trying to understand a complex document written for a specialist audience.
- *The sender and receiver have different expectations.* The words may carry our meaning, but the receiver may be expecting something else from them and interprets accordingly. We may be expecting a promotion at work. We are called into our boss's office, which heightens our expectations — 'this must be it' we think. The boss congratulates us about the handling of a recent matter and the interview ends. We leave the room feeling let down and the boss, no doubt, feels much the same. If we analyse this scenario we can see why the manager might be surprised about the encounter. The manager was giving praise but in return was met with disappointment and a long face. What cannot be known are the thoughts or expectations in someone else's mind.

Oral communications

The greater part of most people's communication is oral. This is as true for the business world as it is in our leisure moments. And yet most people give little thought to their use of the spoken word. A few people take elocution or voice projection and control lessons, but this is usually because they are interested in a career on the stage, rather than because they want to improve their communication skills. Ask the average person how much time they put into training their voice or obtaining feedback about the effect of their voice on others, and they will probably consider you to be a little mad. Your voice and your use of language are parts of your personality but you must not think of them as something fixed — 'something you are born with'. Like your personality, your speaking voice can grow and develop if you want it to.

When you enter the business world you will be expected to take part in an array of situations which call for specialised oral communications. In order to make a success of your business career you need to be prepared to work hard at oral skills. The list of oral skills required for business is long, but for the purposes of illustration some of the more important are listed below:

Taking an active part in committee meetings
Giving speeches and making presentations
Persuading others to our point of view

Negotiating for contracts, deals, etc.
Convincing other people of the worth of your ideas
Selling the company's goods and services
Holding business telephone conversations
Making video presentations
Taking part in appraisal interviews
Holding counselling or welfare interviews
Giving instructions
Training others
Entertaining customers and clients

Each of these situations requires a different set of oral skills, a variety of language use and different ways of speaking. It is only with thought, practice and feedback that the necessary skills can be acquired. Language is a social phenomenon. While people do have private languages with which to communicate with themselves or others close to them, the main purpose of language is to communicate with others. The effectiveness of your oral communication depends on whether your use of language has the desired effect. The questions which follow are designed to help you assess your oral communication skills:

Do other people always listen to what you have to say?
Do other people always understand you and act on your suggestions?
Do you use the right tone and the right words with which to express yourself or do you find yourself tongue-tied?
Are you able to express your emotions and feelings freely when necessary?
Can you confidently speak in a range of different situations, such as on the telephone, while dictating or on video film, and move easily from one to another?
Is your voice loud enough to be heard on all occasions?

Your answers to these questions are important. Without skills such as these, your career progress will be slower than you might hope for. Some of you might hide behind the idea that you are 'shy'. You may be shy, *but good oral communications are a key business skill*. If you are not confident in speaking in a range of different situations then you need practice. You will be given plenty of practice on the course but you must take every opportunity to build on your strengths and overcome your weaknesses. Remember that language is a shared activity and that you will only be able to put your message across if you can speak easily and fluently.

Qualities of speech

Speech is immediate and flexible

Speech is the best medium of communication in many situations. In the vast majority of face-to-face situations we communicate via speech backed up by non-verbal gestures and signs. Speech is, of course, quick and flexible. It is easy to switch from a serious and formal business discussion to a jovial telephone conversation and back again. It allows us to express emotions, explain abstract ideas, ask questions, seek out information, cross-question, tell jokes, make an impression upon others, and a hundred and one other things. Our business and personal lives depend upon being able to use words successfully.

Speech lacks permanence

Although speech is immediate and flexible, it lacks permanence. With modern recording techniques we are able to capture the spoken word but the majority of speech dies as soon as the sound waves our voice creates fade. Speech does, of course, live on in memory but, as we all know, memory can be very unreliable.

For this reason, we need in business to record what has been said. The deliberations of formal committee meetings are always recorded in the form of Minutes. Parliamentary proceedings are written up and published in the daily *Hansard*. It is often useful to make detailed notes after important meetings, interviews and telephone conversations. You will find with experience that this will save endless arguments about what was really said and agreed. Alternatively, you can make an oral record if you have a dictation machine.

Speech provides opportunities for tone and variety

The spoken word has vast opportunities for variety by the use of tone, stress, inflexion and in the way that our words are delivered. Accent, dialect and the register of our voice (whether we use formal or informal language) all add to the variety, as does our use of idioms and colloquialisms.

Accent and dialect can give rise to all sorts of difficulties. Dialects are forms of the language which have certain different words, meanings or sentence constructions from the rest of the language. Dialects like that of the 'Geordies' of north-east England use words like 'canny', 'bairn', 'alreet' in place of those more usually employed in Standard English.

Dialects are spoken with pronounced regional accents. Accents vary the way in which words are pronounced.

English as a language has given rise to a very large number of accents; we recognise national accents for those countries where English is the predominant language — Australian, American, New Zealand, British, Irish accents for example. And within those countries there is a wide variety of accents. This is particularly true of Britain itself.

In Britain, accent has a number of origins which may be regional, social or ethnic. We easily recognise Yorkshire, Scots and Welsh accents, but it is also possible to detect a person's social class by listening to his or her speech. Some accents, like that of London Cockney, are both regional and social. Britain is a country of immigration and many recent immigrant groups speak English with their own accents. It is often possible to tell which part of the world people come from just by listening to them talk, whether it is from Poland, Jamaica, Pakistan or Hong Kong.

There is no one right way of pronouncing or speaking English. Some people believe that 'BBC English' — that form of English properly called 'Received Pronounciation' — is the correct way of speaking. Certainly, received pronounciation does have a dominance in certain circles, particularly in the worlds of the mass media, education and commerce. Because of this cultural dominance it is often seen to be 'proper English' with other ways of speaking judged as inferior. Fortunately, the bias against other accents and dialects has waned in recent years and today they are appreciated for the variety they bring to the language. The important point to bear in mind is — can you be *understood*? Language is a means of communication and if other people cannot understand your speech then you will have to think carefully about modifying the way you speak.

Delivery, tone, intonation and stress are important for adding interest to what we say. The well thought out pause can be used to hold the listener's attention. Stressing important words in a sentence again is an aid to understanding. People will soon stop listening to a monotonous voice. Tone provides the context to the words. Light and humorous delivery for breezy topics, whereas deeper and serious tones for grave and important matters are in order.

Speech allows for colloquialism and slang

Whereas when we write we have to conform to fairly strict rules of grammar, when we speak we have more choice in the way we employ language. All of us have an informal way of speaking when we are with friends and in social settings. We may employ slang terms or colloquialisms — and English has a rich and constantly changing vocabulary of such words and phrases. Some find themselves into formal language while others remain always in the realm of slang. There is nothing wrong with using slang. The important point here, as everywhere, is only to use it when it is appropriate. Some people use informal language as their ordinary language and so run into difficulties when they come up against formal and official situations. In such circumstances their use of slang and informal language may make them seem rather stupid in the eyes of others. Being able to know what is required and when to use particular forms of language is an important skill. You develop it by the subject of our next section — listening.

Listening

When you hear the words *LISTEN* and *LISTENER*, what words do you associate with them? Here is a possible list:

hearing	caring	sympathetic	thought
concentration	attention	trusting	study
understanding	concern	receptive	application
silence	thoughtful	interest	pay heed to

The words in this list are of two types. The first are words which describe the process of listening — hearing, concentration, silence. The second are words which describe the feeling which we have about people who listen. We describe listeners as caring, understanding, trusting and sympathetic individuals.

Listening is an important skill for two reasons. Firstly, it enables you to know and to analyse what others are saying. The better your listening skills the better your understanding of what is being said to you. You will also have a better recall of what has been said. This will mean that you will be in possession of more information and facts than people who pay scant attention to what is being said.

Secondly, if you listen carefully you are more likely to make the right responses to what is being said to you. If you do not listen your responses may be 'off beam' and you may appear to others to be rather stupid. Also, if you listen, people will come to trust you. You will find that people will confide in you and tell you their secrets and unveil their emotions if you are prepared to listen to them. Listeners are usually caring and sympathetic people.

Listening is not just an important communication skill. It is also a major social skill. A person who listens shows that he or she has time for others.

Listening and hearing

There is an important distinction between listening and hearing. We hear a wide range of noises all day and every day but we only listen to those to which we wish to pay attention. Listening is the conscious act of paying attention to a sound. When we listen we analyse, formulate judgements, commit to memory and learn. We are looking for understanding by listening to something or someone. For this reason, listening is an important part of the learning process, and that process should continue throughout life. The development of listening skills is important for your personal and business life.

Improving listening skills

You may say "Surely I do not need to learn how to listen, I have been doing it all my life." Of course you have, but do not confuse hearing with listening. To improve your listening abilities, with all its attendant benefits, you must be prepared to learn how to do it. The following guide may be useful to you. You should:

Set aside times for positive listening practice. As a student you have a perfect opportunity — use your lectures. Radio broadcasts are another good means, but you should also try *listening* to the television. Television is such a visual medium that we all tend to concentrate on the images and not the words. Select a programme and concentrate on the dialogue for a change.

Take notes during your positive listening sessions. Not only do notes provide a record that can be referred to, but they also act as a check on how well you are listening. If you are not listening, you cannot take notes. Make it a habit always to go to a lecture or a meeting with a pen and paper and take notes. Those of you who are taking shorthand units will be doing a lot of listening practice and you will have plenty of opportunities to improve your skills.

Concentrate on what is being said and do not allow yourself to be distracted by whatever else is going on. It is easy to start daydreaming, looking out of the window, or concentrating on other things such as the speaker's facial expressions or clothes. You need to make the effort to put your energy into the task in hand and to listen to what is being said.

Listen with a purpose — why are you listening to this lecture? Set yourself an objective and then use your listening session to achieve it. A useful goal is to obtain maximum benefit out of each lecture or meeting. It is surprising how many people waste their time in class by not concentrating, and then have to go over the same ground again at home. Positive listening is a means of becoming a more effective student.

Enter into the spirit of positive listening. Ask questions during and at the end of classes. This is an excellent way of learning but you can only obtain the material for the questions by listening. Make it your goal to listen in such a way that you ask at least one question by the end of each class. It not only will make the learning more effective but it makes classes more interesting and fun.

Show others that you are listening to them. Facial expressions and body posture can show a speaker that you are listening. A smile, slight nods of the head, laughing at jokes, eye contact, all show the speaker that you care about what you are hearing. This will stimulate the speaker and consequently make your listening more enjoyable. One of the authors once taught a class who applauded at the end of classes they enjoyed. The encouragement given made for a great rapport with the class and gave a stimulus to improve the lectures. It also showed that the class listened. How do you show your appreciation to others for things they do that you have enjoyed?

CHAPTER 5

The Business Letter

One of the essential skills in business is the ability to write clear and informative letters. Despite the use of the telephone and the growing importance of electronic mail, the letter remains the most important communications channel between the business and the outside world.

Why are letters so important and what makes letter writing such a key skill? There are a number of answers to these questions.

The letter is an ambassador for an organisation

Every letter contains a message — it may confirm an order, complain about a late delivery, or clarify a point — but it also does a great deal more. As well as an *explicit* message, a letter contains an *implicit* one. The readers find out about the kind of organisation they are dealing with. A letter plays an ambassadorial role. It is a key means of public relations. The design of the logo and the letterhead, the feel of the paper, the layout of the letter, the quality of the typing and the care with which English is used, all give the reader a message about the organisation they are doing business with. A well-written and crafted letter which is professionally presented will present a positive image both of the writer and of the organisation.

The letter must be able to convey its message to the reader

The purpose of a letter is to convey information and ideas to another person or persons. To do this successfully, care and thought must be given to the choice of words and phrases and to the tone and style.

Letters are a record of what has or has not been agreed or said by various parties

In business, copies of every letter mailed are kept in a file to record what was said and what was agreed. Similarly, letters received are filed for the same purpose. One of the major advantages of letters over telephone conversations is that they provide a permanent record.

What are business letters for?

The purposes for which business letters are used are many but some of the most important are listed below:

- Making complaints.
- Answering letters of complaint (letters of adjustment).
- Making and answering enquiries.
- Requesting and providing information.
- Tendering and confirming quotations.
- Providing references.
- Sending condolences.
- Selling and advertising (mail-shots).
- Providing introductions.
- Applying for jobs.
- Requesting payment.

Stationery

All organisations use printed stationery. The reasons for this are simple but important:

- Printed stationery saves time and effort by not having to reproduce standard material such as addresses and telephone numbers.
- Printed stationery ensures that every item of correspondence conforms to the requirements of the law.
- Printed stationery provides a means of projecting the organisation's image to its customers and clients.
- Printed stationery ensures that there is a degree of conformity in the correspondence which leaves the organisation.

Corporate identity and logos

An essential element of the layout is the printed format of the paper, known as the *letterhead*. Nowadays, the printing is not just confined to the head of the paper. The purpose of the letterhead is to produce a *corporate identity*. This is to give a particular impression of the organisation to its public. It is usual for a company to have a policy on its corporate image and to carry this image through to all its publicly available printed materials such as price lits, brochures and leaflets, visiting cards, compliments slips, envelopes and display boards and signs.

The most important part of the corporate identity, after the name of the organisation itself, is the *logo*. A logo is a visual symbol which seeks to communicate a simple message to the public in such a way that it is instantly recognisable and memorable. Just try thinking of Coca Cola or Pepsi Cola and you probably think of their distinctive logos. The publishers of this book, Macmillan Education, use a large M as their logo and you will find it displayed on the base of the spine of this book. Virtually every organisation, large or small, uses a logo to express its identity to the public. Your College will have its logo on its prospectus, application forms and headed letter paper. It is usual to design a logo around the organisation's name or an abbreviation of it.

Activity: 'Logos'

You should design a series of logos for your College, its Department of Business Studies, and for three or four of the companies prominent in your area. Do not worry that they already have logos. In addition to the actual design, you should include a short statement of why you chose a particular design, what message it seeks to convey, and the type of image it is portraying.

Statutory requirements

The law has a deal to say about what information should be contained on a business letter. The person receiving a letter from a company must be given a degree of information about the organisation which they are dealing with.

The nature of the legal requirement depends upon the type of organisation it is. Sole traders and partnerships must conform with the *Business Names Act* 1985. This states that the following information must be given in legible characters on all business letters, written orders, invoices, receipts and demands for payment:

- The name of each partner, if the business is a partnership.
- The name of the individual carrying on a business as a sole trader.

Companies must comply with the *Companies Act* 1985 and display the following information on their stationery:

- The company's name.
- The company's place of registration and the number with which it is registered.
- The address of the registered office.
- Its status as a limited company — for example, Ltd, Plc. For any limited company exempt from the obligation to use the word 'limited' as part of its name, the fact that it is a limited company. This normally applies to private companies limited by guarantee. The Business and Technician Education Council is such a company and you should ask your course tutor to see one of their communications to see how they display their limited liability status.
- Companies do not have to list their directors on their stationery, but if they do they must list the full name (or the surname and initials of forenames) of every individual and corporate director.

Other essential information and stationery style

In addition to the requirement to conform to the law, all business stationery should usually display the following information:

- The address of the company, including the postcode (or the address of the branch, factory or site to which replies should be sent).
- The telephone, telex and fax numbers.
- References. The company's reference is usually marked Our ref:, the customer's as Your ref:.

With so much information required in a business letter, the style of the printed material is of importance. The style needs to be clear, uncluttered, informative and one that projects the company image in a positive fashion. The other essential is to make certain that there is sufficient space on which the text of the letter can be typed. The last point sounds simple but some organisations do become so carried away with logos and elaborate art work that well over half the area of the printed page is unavailable for typed material. There are organisations which prefer plain matter of fact styles, while others favour elaborate designs and layouts. It is becoming a measure of good practice to find an uncluttered style and not to overburden stationery with heavy dark ink and dominating logos. To create this light style, the company address and other essential information can be relegated to the bottom of the page. This leaves just the name and the logo, or perhaps just the logo at the top of the sheet.

How to lay out a business letter

There are a number of conventions which you need to master for laying out a business letter. You should note that there is no single correct business letter layout. The convention you follow may be a matter of personal choice but nowadays it is more likely to be a matter of company house-style. An organisation will specify that all its letters must be typewritten on headed paper and use, say, a *fully blocked, open punctuation style*. If you work for an organisation which dictates a house-style, then you must conform to it in your correspondence, but you should remember that there are a number of equally valid alternatives.

The conventions of letter writing, like the conventions of language, change. The changes reflect altering taste and also developments in technology. Word processors, electronic typewriters and printers tend to favour certain layouts over others.

Style of punctuation

Typewritten business letters have different conventions to handwritten letters. The main difference is that a style has evolved known as *open punctuation* in which *all* punctuation outside of the main body of the letter is omitted. Letters which are traditionally punctuated are said to have a *closed punctuation* style.

Open punctuation is a very popular style in business letters. The reasons are based on both economy and style. It saves time and effort on the part of the typist not to have to put commas at the end of each and every line of an address and full stops at the end of an address and after the date. In addition, open punctuation makes the page look neater, cleaner and crisper.

Blocked and semi-blocked format

There are two conventions of layout in common use — *semi-blocked* and the more modern *fully blocked* format. Remember, neither format is more correct than the other. The choice of layout is a question of style and preference.

The *semi-blocked* letter (see figure 3) has the following features:

- The date is situated on the right-hand side of the page in line with the address.
- The paragraphs are indented, usually five spaces from the left-hand margin.

JFB

JFB Marketing Ltd.,
47 Palmers Court,
Crainton Street,
London WC13 6CT.

01 853 15437

22nd January 19. .

Your ref:
Our ref:

Mr. D. Loman,
73 Bell Lane,
London SW3 16RW.

Dear Mr. Loman,

....
....

....
....
....
....

....
....
....

Yours sincerely,

V. A. Holt.
Sales Manager.

Registered Offices   58 Stamford Road, London WC1 6PF.
Registered in England No. 12345698

Figure 3   Semi-blocked format

- The complimentary close (yours sincerely/yours faithfully) is centred on the page.
- The signature and the sender's name and title are centred.
- The layout is fully punctuated.

JFB Marketing Ltd
47 Palmers Court
Crainton   Street
London WC13 6CT

01   853   15437

Your ref
Our ref

22nd January 19..

Mr D Loman
73 Bell Lane
London SW3 6RW

Dear Mr Loman

....
....

....
....
....
....

....
....
....

Yours sincerely

V A Holt
Sales Manager

Registered Offices   58 Stamford Street, London WC1 6PF
Registered in England No. 12345698

Figure 4   Fully blocked format

The *fully blocked* letter (see figure 4) has the following features:

- All typing begins on the left-hand margin.
- The date is typed on the left-hand margin.

- The layout will use open punctuation (that is, no punctuation). This is done for neatness of presentation. The content of the letter is punctuated.

There is a half-way house style known as the *blocked format* which starts all paragraphs on the left-hand side margin but leaves the date on the right and centres the complimentary close.

Salutations and complimentary closes

It is a strong convention to link the recipient's name and address to a particular salutation and complimentary close. The usual practice is as follows:

If you are addressing a named person or persons — Joan Johnson, Mr A. B. Tiller, Mr and Mrs Smith — then the salutation will address them by name.

> *Dear Mrs Johnson* or *Dear Joan* (depending on how well you know the person you are writing to)

If you are writing to a woman whose marital status you are unaware of, then the title *Ms* can be used.

The complimentary close when addressing a named person(s) is *Yours sincerely*. A letter addressed to a close acquaintance — Dear John — can close with *Kind regards* or *Best Wishes*.

If you are addressing an organisation or a person known only to you by their title — the Head of Business Studies, The Metal Consortium PLC, the Department of Health and Social Security — then the salutation will be *Dear Madam* if the recipient is known to be a woman and, traditionally, Dear Sir if the sex is unknown. However, with so many women holding important positions we prefer the use of Dear Sir or Madam. This shows consideration to the recipient.

Such letters will close with *Yours faithfully*.

References

It makes a great deal of sense to include a reference on all business letters. Most business letters have printed on them

> Our ref: (refers to outgoing mail)
> Your ref: (refers to incoming mail)

The reason is to be able with ease to identify the sender of the letter, who typed it, and the file number if the organisation has one for a particular account. Without references, letters may do the rounds of various desks before the correct destination is found. This means that there will be a delay in dealing with the correspondence, which is bad for the sender, but also puts the organisation in a poor light.

The convention which usually governs references is to include the writer's initials followed by the initials of the person who typed it — ES/NS. This may be followed by an account reference number ES/NS 17360/N/164.

The recipients of the letter

On all business letters, the name (where known), title and address of the recipient of the letter is included. This is to make it clear to whom the letter is intended, to ensure that the recipient has an address for further correspondence, and to provide the address for window envelopes if they are being used.

Subject heading

Many writers add a subject heading to a letter on the line immediately below the salutation. The reason for this is so that the recipient can see at a glance what the letter is about. Most business people receive so much correspondence that it is difficult for them to deal with all their correspondence immediately on receipt. Subject heading can be a guide to the importance of the content.

Dear Miss Hughes
Installation of a Photocopier

Designation and signature

Letters are always signed. In some organisations all letters have to go out under the signature of a senior manager while in others designated employees can sign their own letters. It is important for the recipient to know the name and the status of the sender of correspondence. Because a signature may be difficult to decipher, the sender's name and title are always typed at the end of the letter.

You may have received a letter where the letters p.p. are written before the signature of the sender. This means that the letter has been signed by another — the secretary or personal assistant — in the absence of their principal.

Figure 5 shows a general completed layout for a business letter.

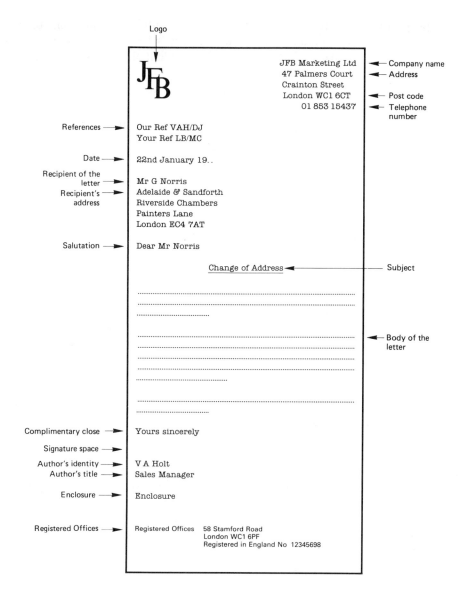

Figure 5

Confidentiality

It is often the case that a letter is for the eyes of a particular person and nobody else. The usual practice in most offices is for a post-clerk or secretary to open all the incoming mail and to place it in the in-tray of the appropriate recipient. If this is the case with confidential material, then there can be no guarantee that the secrecy of the material can be maintained. To avoid this happening, confidential mail should have CONFIDENTIAL printed on the envelope and on the letter itself. The latter is to remind the recipient of the letter's status.

Some organisations have a hierarchy of confidentiality — CONFIDENTIAL, PRIVATE & CONFIDENTIAL, STRICTLY CON- FIDENTIAL, TOP SECRET.

If you are sending a personal letter to a person at their place of employment and you wish that person only to open it, the envelope and letter should be marked PERSONAL.

Writing the letter

So far we have discussed the conventions of the layout of letters. We now turn to the important business of composing appropriate letters.

We will start with the *structure of the letter*. A business letter, like any piece of writing, will be best structured by working to a plan. This will help ensure that the information will be presented in a sensible and logical order and that the necessary information is included.

The opening of the letter

A well-written business letter will start by putting its message into context. The use of a subject heading is an aid to this. It should be followed by stating the reason why the letter is being written and by acknowledging any previous correspondence. Many openings are of a standard variety:

> Thank you for your letter of the 17th February 19 . . concerning . . .
> I have received your letter of . . .
> I am replying to your letter of . . .

All of these introductions are personal and to the point. Some writers employ the words 'reference' in some form such as 'With reference to your letter . . . '. This is not recommended as it is impersonal. Worse still is the use of the shortened form of reference 're' as in 'Re your letter of . . . '. Even in a formal business letter you should use a personal and human form of address.

Of course, not all business letters are in reply to someone else's letter. You may be initiating the correspondence. If this is the case then the opening sentence must make your purpose clear:

I am applying for the post of . . .
I wish to place an order for . . .
I have pleasure in informing you of . . .

The body of the letter

The middle paragraph(s) of the letter gives the details of the business which has been introduced in the opening paragraph. It may be the detailed description and prices of merchandise, details of a complaint, ideas for a new product, or whatever. The important point is to write the information in a clear and logical fashion. To help you do this it is useful to:

- Keep sentences short. It is easier to think clearly with short sentences than long ones. Long sentences can become complicated and so obscure the message.
- Use tabulated formats if you have a number of points to make.
- Do not use unnecessary words. 'I will be brief and to avoid further confusing the issue I intend . . . ' — this is a trap which many writers fall into. Phrases such as 'I must emphasise the importance . . . ', 'I would also add . . . ', are a waste of words and best avoided. Come straight to the point and keep to the point are the golden rules of letter writing.
- Do not say more than you have to.
- Do not confuse your reader with technical terms or jargon. If you have to use technical terms and you have any reason to believe that your reader may not understand them, then you should explain them.
- Be careful in your choice of words. If you can pick between a common and a less common word, always choose the common one. Never show off in your use of words. It does not impress the reader and it may obscure the message.

Concluding the letter

You need to make it clear to the recipient what it is you want of them. This is the purpose of the letter's concluding paragraph:

Please deliver the goods to our Manchester office.
I expect the matter to be dealt with promptly.
Thank you, again, for inviting me.

It is usual to have a closing pleasantry, but you should only use them if they add to the letter in a positive manner:

Please let me know if I can be of further assistance.
Do not hesitate to contact me if you require more information.

Tone and style

It is important to use language appropriately in business correspondence.
You cannot be informal when giving notice of dismissal or redundancy, or
if you are writing a letter of condolence or complaint. On the other hand a
close business acquaintance will be surprised to receive a letter from you
with a very formal tone. There are a number of points to keep in mind
when considering the appropriate style and tone of business letters:

- Make certain that the style suits the subject. If you are asking a favour
  you must be polite. A complaint requires a forceful approach. An
  order for goods should be factual and to the point. A conciliatory tone
  should be adopted for a letter of adjustment.
- Keep the reader in mind. If you know the recipient, then your letter
  should be shaped to his or her personality and status. This is particularly important if you have to convey technical information to someone
  you know not to be an expert.
  It is easy to make the mistake of sounding pompous in business
  letters. If you are clear who you are writing to and address them
  directly, the tone of your letter has a good chance of appropriately
  expressing your message.
- Let your letter express your personality. Business letters do not need
  always to be impersonal and formal. If you are genuinely pleased to
  hear of someone's success, then say so. If you are pleased to do
  business with a customer, then let the customer know of your pleasure.
- You should be polite, tactful and helpful whenever possible. It is easy
  to sound harsh and uncaring by using impersonal language. If you are
  sorry that you cannot be of assistance, then you should say so. If you
  can provide help and assistance in ways which are beneficial to a
  customer or client, then you should always do so. And if you have to
  break an appointment or point out an error, then it is important to use
  phrases which are tactful and polite.

> "I am sorry to inform you that we no longer carry a stock of the
> spare parts you require. I believe that A. J. Northwood & Sons is
> the closest dealer who may be able to help you. Their address
> is . . . "
> "Please accept my apologies for having to cancel our meeting on
> the 24th January. A matter has arisen requiring my personal
> attention. I will phone you next week to arrange another date."

"I am sorry to inform you that your application for the post of . . . has been unsuccessful."

Standard letters and paragraphs

You may find yourself writing a large number of similar letters on a regular basis. If this is the case, then you may wish to compose a number of standard letters which can be sent as a matter of routine. With the advent of word processors, the use of standard letters and paragraphs has been made easier. But there are dangers as well as benefits to their use.

Many people in business mark their correspondence with a series of letters and numbers which are instructions to the typist to compose a letter from previously composed standard paragraphs.

A note on a piece of correspondence may read as follows — 'A (insert 12th March), B, D & E'. Each letter would refer to a standard paragraph, although in paragraph A there is the need for the insertion of a date.

Standard letters of this kind are very useful as replies to stock enquiries. A standard paragraph may not always reflect the tone required to deal with a particular enquiry; it may not be quite appropriate to particular circumstances and it may not feel right to the recipient. Therefore, while there are many advantages in standard letters, they should be used with caution.

Activity: 'Letter writing'

1. Many of us become hot under the collar over local issues, whether it is poor transport services, an objection to the proposed siting of an amusement arcade opposite where we live, or the lack of sports and other social facilities. Read the letters page of your local newspaper and become acquainted with the style, manner and length of letters written by other citizens. When you have done this, compose a letter stating your views on an issue of your choice and with the intention of publication in your local paper.
2. Your knowledge of organisations can always be improved by visits to see particular processes or operations in action. Choose a business in your area which interests you and about whose products or services you would like to know more. Write a letter to its Publicity Department requesting a visit and stating what it is you want to see and what you are hoping to find out. Do not forget to include details of dates and times when you will be free to make your visit.

3. As the end of your course approaches you will begin making job applications. Preparation is one of the keys to success. Using national newspapers, select at least one job which is of interest to you and then write a letter of application.
4. The authors would welcome constructive comments and suggestions about this book and, in particular, about the various 'activities' contained in it. Write a letter to us 'c/o' our Publisher.

The Memorandum

The memo is the life blood of the communications system of the organisation. It is the main form of *internal* business correspondence and the means used to communicate the majority of written messages. Most memos are still paper memos but increasingly they are sent electronically via computer networks.

The word 'memorandum' means a message which aids the memory. As you will find out, they can be used for a variety of purposes and memos are produced in a number of formats. The flexibility of the memo makes it the major form of internal communication.

The format of the memo

Brief memos are usually written on A5 size paper (148 × 210 millimetres) and larger and more complicated ones on A4 size paper (210 × 297 millimetres).

The following tables give the defining features of memos:

Format	*Notes*
To	The receiver(s)
From	The sender(s)
Copies	Often copies of memos are sent to other people for their reference. The receiver must know who else is acquainted with the memo's contents
Reference	A memo may carry a reference which may consist of the sender's and typist's initials and/or a reference number

Date	Memos act as a record and must be dated
Subject	It is usual to write a short title to each memo in order that the reader can see what it is about at a glance
The Message	This should be as short as practicable, clear and to the point. The use of a note format with numbered paragraphs helps to reduce reading time and aids understanding
Reply	Memos are often sent on pre-printed forms, many of which are divided in two. The message is written on the left-hand side. The receiver can write a reply on the right
Signature(s)	In some organisations it is the practice to sign memos.

An example is shown in figure 6.

```
                        Memorandum

To:    All Departmental Managers          Date:  16th February 19..
                                          Ref:   AS/LH
Copies: Company Secretary

From:  Head of Building Services

Subject: CAR PARKING DISCS

Message:                          | Reply:                Date;

The problem of employees parking  |
cars in the underground car park  |
without displaying discs is causing|
serious difficulties for the car park|
attendant. Would all Managers inform|
their staff of the necessity of properly|
displayed discs. Please provide me with|
the names and car registration    |
numbers of any of your staff who do|
not have discs. I need this information|
by the 20th February so that I can|
issue the additional discs as quickly as|
possible.                         |

          Signature:              |        Signature:
```

Figure 6

What are memos used for?

To inform others

They can be used to inform others of a wide variety of matters.

To record Company policy decisions

These are often communicated via official memorandums. Some organisations colour-code their memos and have, say, yellow for policy memos, blue for information and white for all others.

To seek information

Many memos are written to find out information from within the organisation.

To place views on record

It is often the case that a member of an organisation wishes to put views or ideas on record. This can best be done by means of a written memo.

To confirm conversations and telephone conversations

A memo is a clear means of recording the outcome of an oral discussion.

To give instructions

It is the case that, in all organisations, instructions need to be communicated. The issuing of memos is a common means of give instructions.

Style

As memos are often short and written to others within the same organisation, the style that a memo is written in is not thought to matter. In some situations, such as providing purely factual information, this may be the case, but insensitive memos have been known to have an adverse effect on the motivation of others and their willingness to carry out instructions.

The style which is employed will depend upon the intention of the writer:

- *Information giving*
  Memos which provide straightforward information can be written in an impersonal and formal style. If the fire drill procedure is being altered, or the opening times of the staff canteen are being extended, then a

factual style is appropriate. Memos of this type are often displayed on notice boards for general information.

- *Information seeking*
  The style for information giving is too often confused with information seeking. The latter involves the recipient of the memo in additional work, whereas merely giving information does not. When you want other people to do things for you, then style should be polite and you may need to persuade them to co-operate. It is important to explain why the information is required. Far too often those in authority expect others to obey and so use formal and even terse language when penning memos. Subordinates will respond — they have to — but will do so in bad grace if they feel that they are not being properly treated.

- *Directing*
  There are a few occasions where it is absolutely necessary to issue a general instruction. Formal language is required, and it may be necessary to state the consequences if the memo's contents are not complied with. Nevertheless, it is still possible to request co-operation and compliance with the instructions in a polite way.

- *Communicating ideas*
  Memos are often used to put forward a view or to provide new thinking on a subject. If you are writing memos of this type, the language can be personal and lively in order to communicate the freshness of your views. Other people need to be excited by new approaches and this cannot be achieved by a dull and formal memorandum.

- *Motivating others*
  Memos are sometimes used to help motivate others. It may be that last year's sales figures were up and you want to stimulate others to greater efforts. Again, lively and vivid language is best employed for this end.

- *Personal communication*
  Often people who know each other well communicate by memo. If only the two people are involved in the communication then an informal and personal style is the rule. However, if the memo is to be copied to others or is likely to 'go public', then a more formal tone may need to be employed.

Activity: 'Writing memos'

1. How much do you know about the structure of your College? Write a memo to the Principal requesting an interview to discuss the College organisation.
2. What do you know about departments within the College, other than your own? Write a memo to the Head of Catering/Engineering/Building or any other Department, requesting an interview to discuss the courses offered and the careers that they are expected to lead to.
3. How much do you know about your own Department? Write a memo, to be pinned on the college notice board, offering to pass that knowledge on to other students.
4. Write a memo to the Head of your Department suggesting social and/or sports events which you think would improve college life.

Using the Telephone

How often do you use the telephone? Most people now have a telephone at home and many more use telephones in their working lives. Businesses would have difficulty surviving without the use of this communication tool, and our private lives would be very different without it.

It is possible to dial a number and, within seconds, to be speaking to a business acquaintance or friend in Saudi Arabia, the USA or Australia, to name just three of the many countries it is possible to dial direct. By dialling three digits it is possible to call for emergency help from the police, fire and ambulance services in addition to being able to ask for sea, mountain or cave rescue. We can call operator services if we are unable to locate the number of someone we wish to contact or if we are having difficulty in making the desired connection. It is possible to book alarm calls, make transferred charge calls, telephone for travel information, for the time, the weather, or just to listen to a story or some music! The telephone system is becoming increasingly flexible, allowing telephone calls to be made almost anywhere. Car phones and portable telephones are now common-place. Many businesses employ telephone conferencing as a convenient means of holding meetings. There are many more services available from our telephone system — many of which we take for granted. In fact, we probably take the whole system of communication by telephone very much for granted.

Using the telephone has become a 'habit' for many people. Have you noticed how well-prepared some individuals are when they answer the phone and how others are ill-prepared, as though they never receive calls? What makes some people 'better' on the telephone than others? Let us take a look at this phenomenon. Some voices are miserable and unfriendly while others are so happy and bright we can hear 'the smile' in them. Which would you rather talk to? A good telephone voice does not mean having a middle class or 'posh' accent — it means developing a friendly, happy and interesting tone, and adjusting the pitch of your voice to suit the situation. A good telephone voice can do much to improve the temper of irate or unhappy callers.

Activity: 'Smiling voices'

Spend one whole day concentrating on the sound of your voice. However you feel, make an effort to sound happy every time you speak. You will be surprised at how people will respond to you, and their reaction will encourage you to be happy and to continue speaking with 'a smile' in *your* voice.

Receiving calls

There are many other ways in which our telephone technique can be improved. Here are some of them:

- Always answer the telephone promptly.
- Always answer with a greeting and any relevant information, such as "Good morning! Sallis and Sallis, can I help you?" or "Hello! Extension 007, Jane Bond speaking."
- Always answer the phone clearly and say who you are — "Jane Murphy, can I help you" or "Good morning, Murphy speaking, can I be of assistance." Do *not* say "Mr Smith" or "Miss Jones." Other people use titles to address you but you should not use a title, only your name.
- Always have a pad and pen next to your telephone — and encourage others to do the same. Telephone message forms are even better than a pad as they prevent you from forgetting to ask relevant questions. Having to say "hold on while I find a pen" to a caller always makes an organisation appear to be inefficient.
- Always write messages down at once, and read them back to the caller so that they can be checked.
- Always give the caller ample time to explain the reason for the call.
- Always keep the caller informed of what is happening — they cannot see you!
- Always give the caller your undivided attention.
- Always treat the caller in the way in which you would hope to be treated.
- Always be patient.
- Never keep callers waiting while you look for information or try to transfer them, etc., without explaining what you are doing and giving them a chance to call back if they are in a hurry or if they are calling long-distance.
- Never use slang or jargon.

- Never lose your temper.
- Never shout.

Making calls

Remember that a telephone call costs your employer both money and time, and for those reasons your technique for making calls should be both planned and cost-effective. One important element in this is to make certain that you understand the tariff for calls and that you only make essential calls during peak rate periods.

As with any other aspect of business, proper planning and thought will improve your technique and reduce the possibility of errors and misunderstandings. It will keep the cost of calls to a minimum. The following pointers will help you improve your technique for making calls:

- Plan your call thoroughly before you make it. Be certain who you want to talk to, what you want to say, and whether you want to leave a message if he or she is not available. It is a good idea to jot the points down on paper before you dial the number.
- Make certain that you have any letters, your diary, files, and any other necessary documentation available if you need to refer to them. Searching for papers can be annoying to the person being called and it wastes time and money.
- Make certain that you are not disturbed when making a call and that there is the minimum of background interference.
- Always have a pen and paper by the phone so that you are able to take notes of the conversation. You should write up the notes immediately after the call before the memory of the call fades (see figure 7)
- Dial the number carefully as this will reduce the likelihood of a wrong number or a misdirected call.
- When you are connected, be clear and confident in your manner when you are asking for the person you want to speak to and in announcing yourself:
     "Good afternoon, this is Kate Farmer from Witcombe & Co. I wish to speak to Mrs Cooke please."
- Be prepared for a delay while the operator puts you through to the relevant extension. In many organisations you will be put through to a secretary whose job it is to filter calls. In order to pass through the barrier you will need to explain the nature of your message briefly, although if it is confidential you must say so. If the person you want to speak to is not available, then you should leave a clear and precise message. You should make it clear whether you will phone back or whether you wish to be telephoned.

- When you make your calls, ensure that you speak clearly and precisely. Pay attention to your intonation and emphasis.
- Be careful about the way you pronounce names and figures. You may need to spell them out or check that they have been understood. Seek confirmation that the other party understands your meaning.
- Do not make unnecessarily long calls as they are wasteful. On the other hand, do take the trouble to be friendly and courteous. A telephone conversation allows the opportunity to build up a personal relationship.

PHONE MESSAGE

Date: *8th January 19..*   **Message:** *Sharon Fox*

Time: *1415*   **For:** *Accounts Dept.*

Caller: *John Coe*

Tel. no.: *0893 73129 ext 46*

Address: _____

_____

Message *Mr. Coe will be able to*

attend the meeting on

Thursday 14th January, but

please phone him tomorrow

to confirm the time

Message taken by: *Doreen Smith*

Figure 7

Report Writing

A business report can either be written or oral. In it an employee may be required to analyse a given situation, comment on progress made to date, provide advice and possibly to make recommendations.

There is no standard form for reports. The style and format will depend upon the content and the context of the report and the audience to whom it is addressed. Usually, when a person is asked to provide a report he or she is given a brief which provides the terms of reference. There are some organisations which have standard report forms, and these are designed to save writers' and readers' time. Report forms are particularly useful for standard reports such as accident or progress reports.

It is important to keep your audience in mind when writing a report. It should be designed to meet the readers' needs and to solve their problems. The form of a report should allow you to put your ideas across to your readers.

Types of report

Reports for the public

> Annual Reports
> Press Releases

Reports for a specific audience

> References
> Disciplinary Report
> Staff Report/Annual Appraisal Record

Routine reports

> Maintenance Report
> Inspection Report
> Quality Control Report
> Production Report
> Sales Report

Occasional reports

> Accident Reports

Commissioned reports

> Market Research findings
> Fact-finding Surveys
> Investigating/Research Reports
> Policy Change and Revision Reports

Oral reports

These are generally used when speed is of the essence, but you may be called upon to give an oral report to accompany a written one. This will usually involve summarising the main points, findings and conclusions of the written report.

Writing a report

Whatever the purpose and the format of the report you are writing, there is one common thread running through all of them. You must be able to put your message across in a clear and lucid manner. This is a difficult art but the following simple guidelines can ease the process. The key to writing clearly is to know what you want to say and, in order to do that, you need a plan to which to write.

Terms of reference

When you are asked to write a report you will be given terms of reference, for example:

> "Please provide me by the 16th May with a detailed written Report on why during the past year the volume of customer complaints rose by 15%. I will expect you to make recommendations which will seek to eliminate the causes of the complaints."

Occasionally, you may write a report on your own initiative, and in this case you must set out your own terms of reference.

Drawing up a plan

You need to list the points you intend to cover and put them in order. Decide on the length of the report and its format. You need to work out in advance what it is you want to say.

Defining your audience

You must know whom you are writing for. Different groups demand different styles of writing. Do your readers understand the background and context of your subject? If they do, then you can concentrate on the matters at hand. If they do not, then you must provide them with an explanation of why the report is being written.

Is your readership composed of experts or not? You can use technical jargon for experts but lay people will require explanations and your skill will be in putting technical matters into everyday language.

Writing as you speak

The key to a clear style of writing is to write as you speak. You should imagine your readers and write as if you were speaking to them. This will help your presentation to be clear and direct. It will prevent your report from being cluttered and long winded.

Remember, if you want to convince people to do something, then your report must be persuasive. If you want to inform them, then it must be communicative. Decide what it is you want to do with the report and choose a style which is appropriate.

Writing clearly and concisely

Choose words which best convey your message to your audience. You are fortunate to be writing in English as your language has a vocabulary of over half a million words — over five times as many as French. This gives you choice and so you should aim to pick words which accurately and concisely convey your meaning. It generally aids understanding to use short words rather than long ones. A *Thesaurus* will help you find appropriate words and assist your composition by providing a choice of words. In fact, this is its main function.

Structure of reports

From what we have said above it is clear that there is no single structure for reports, although what follows can be used as a model:

1. Terms of Reference.
2. Summary of main findings and conclusions.
3. Introduction. Sets the scene and explains the nature and purpose of the report.
4. The Body of the Report. This is a detailed description of the evidence, the methods used and the research findings.
5. Conclusions and Results. This draws together the findings from the body of the report.
6. Recommendations. This is the important part of the report as it is the reason for the original commissioning of the report. You need to show how the recommendations follow from the conclusions drawn from the relevant evidence.
7. Appendices. These contain detailed statistical or other information which would disturb the flow if presented in the body of the report.

Activity: 'Report writing'

1. Write a report for your Course Tutor on the last industrial visit which your group made. The report should be between 750 and 1000 words in length and contain an explanation of what you learnt from the visit.
2. Write a report for the Head of your Department on your experiences (a) on your course and (b) at the College. You should pay particular attention to the differences between your experience of school and that of College.
3. Write a report of between 1000 and 1500 words on your last period of work experience with particular emphasis on the benefit it has been to you. The report is to be written for the Personnel Officer of the organisation which provided you with the placement.

CHAPTER 9

Press Releases

Many organisations use press releases because it provides them with publicity at little or no cost. Newspapers and radio stations use them as copy for stories, as this unsolicited material is a good source of news for little effort. Reporters cannot be everywhere and so press releases can help to ensure that newsworthy events receive the publicity they deserve.

> *The art of a good press release is to excite the editor's interest with the first sentence. It is important to use the first few sentences to summarise the story you are presenting.*

If the story is newsworthy enough a newspaper or radio station will use it, however dull and uninteresting the press release. But you stand a better chance of your material being used if it is topical, lively and written in a similar style to that employed by the particular newspaper or radio station. You must first seek to interest the editor and to do this you must make certain that the essence of the story is contained in the first few sentences. You cannot guarantee that an editor will read to the end of a press release.

Writing a press release

Remember that with any piece of writing you must address a particular audience. This is especially true of press releases. You should be very careful in your choice of intended audiences. Is your story one of general interest or is it a specialist story which is destined for, say, the business page of the local paper? If it is the latter kind, then you can be rather more technical and detailed than you might be for the general readership.

Remember that the general public is looking for newsworthy stories. In order to read the story they must find it interesting or useful, and it must not be so detailed and technical that they cannot understand it. Stories are more eye-catching if they refer to particular people rather than to abstract ideas or impersonal facts.

'Managing Director tells of bright future'

has more appeal than

'The growth in planned production is to be 15% greater than that in the last financial year'

Once you have attracted people's attention to a story with a bright, lively opening paragraph, you can provide them with some facts and figures. There is always a danger in becoming too technical. A good way of breaking up the detailed explanation is to add a quotation or two in this section. This again provides a personal angle as well as a change of style.

'The company's plan is to relocate its main offices to a five acre green field site. The relocation will be in three phases, each of which is planned to take eighteen months. In all, some 300 people will be involved in the move. One of those who is first to move, Mrs Jean Cooke, a secretary in the Sales Department, said, "I have seen the plans for new offices and it is going to be super. The offices are going to be bright and airy. I am looking forward to the move." '

The quotation from Mrs Cooke is important. Many people who work in offices may identify with her and envy her new working conditions. She sounds motivated and this may lead other people to consider to apply for jobs with the company. Potential customers may like the sound of doing business with such enthusiastic people. Mrs Cooke will have friends and relations who will buy papers to see her name in print.

Sentences in press releases should be kept short. It is usual in popular journalism to write short sentences and to use clear, everyday language. You should follow this convention in writing a press release.

Always leave the least important part of the story until the end. At first sight this might sound a little strange. You may feel that the last paragraph should be a strong conclusion, but you must remember the realities of the news room and the editor's desk. Your release may be 600 words but, if the editor can only print a story of 400, the easiest means of editing is to cut the last part of the story.

You should, of course, present the press release properly. It should be typed on A4 paper with double spacing and generous margins. The idea is to give the editor plenty of room to make changes and alterations.

Sending appropriate photographs can help the press release's chances of being published although, if a picture helps the telling of the story, the newspaper will usually prefer to have its own photographer take pictures.

Figure 8 shows what a press release might look like.

PENNINGTON BROTHERS
58 Aldershot Road
Watchet, Hants HA3 7UT.

PRESS RELEASE

Success for Simon

Simon Townsend at the age of 25 has become the youngest departmental manager at Pennington Brothers. The local specialist tool makers have just promoted him to lead their Accounts Department.

He has worked for Pennington's since he left school. Accountancy first interested him in his day-release business studies course at Woking Technical College. He transferred to Accounts from Sales and has never looked back.

Managing Director, John Leslie, has nothing but praise for Simon. "He has worked hard. We helped him with day-release but he gained his accountancy qualification entirely by correspondence study. Our policy is to promote bright, young people wherever possible. Simon's success is a tribute to his hard work and dedication to his work".

Many local people in Evering, Simon's home town, will know him for more than figures at Pennington's. In his spare time he heads the local scout group and is an enthusiastic member of the dramatic society.

End

Encl. Photograph of Simon
Townsend

For further details, contact
Heather Perryman on
578 63217 ext 238

Figure 8

Activity: Designing a press release

Would you like to see your group's name in the local paper? If so, why not draft a press release and send it to the local press describing their achievements? There must be a great deal which you are involved in which will be of interest to the general public.

CHAPTER 10

Visual Presentation of Information

Today it is commonplace to find business reports and academic textbooks employing complicated statistical and numerical data in interesting visual forms. You may not realise that this is quite a recent phenomenon. If you look at most textbooks of ten or fifteen years ago in your library, you will find that they contain mainly text. Few books are published nowadays without the authors using graphics to illustrate their ideas. This is particularly true when it comes to material requiring numerical analysis. Not only textbook writers are utilising such methods. Companies are very aware that effective presentation is a major means of marketing their image.

Company reports and brochures are often very good sources of pictorial presentation. Internal reports are also becoming better illustrated, and therefore more informative, through the introduction of *desk top publishing*. This is the name given to integrated computer hardware and software which allows for the easy production in the office of complex and elaborate documents and reports. The software packages allow for bar charts and pictograms to be easily incorporated into the body of a report, while a high-quality laser printer doubles as a photocopier so that large numbers of perfect copies can be easily produced.

Visual presentations catch the eye and make the reader interested in reading the accompanying text. This is especially true when figures are being presented. Comparisons are simpler to make when numerical data is presented in diagrammatic form and conclusions are easier to draw from it.

This chapter is not about statistics. You will cover statistical and quantitative methods elsewhere on your course. Instead, it is designed to assist you in considering how charts and diagrams can make the presentation of data more interesting and informative. Whenever you want to show a trend, analyse large amounts of data or highlight statistical information in a report, then graphs and charts are the ideal means of presentation.

Thinking in pictures

Look at the following:

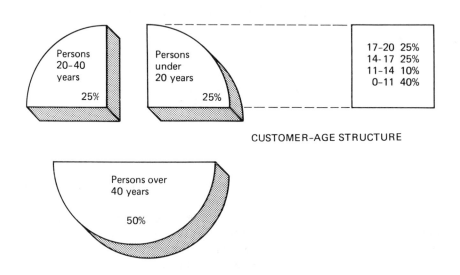

CUSTOMER-AGE STRUCTURE

The information in this *exploded pie diagram* is presented in a clear and effective way. The same data is given in a different format in the paragraph which follows:

> "The age structure of our customers as provided by the latest survey is as follows — approximately 50% of them are over 40 years; some 25% are in the 20–40 age group; while the remaining 25% are aged below 20 years. Of the under 20s — 40% are aged under 11; 10% are in the 11–14 age bracket; 25% are 14–17; and the remaining 25% are aged 17–20 years."

If you read the paragraph carefully you will find your eyes continually moving to the pie chart for confirmation that you have understood what has been written. The information in both is identical; it is only the format which is different. But because one format is visual, this makes it easier to comprehend and understand. Visual formats make the drawing of conclusions simpler. The continuous text is dull and, therefore, difficult to read. This makes it hard to use the information it provides constructively. The choice of format is not merely one of preference, it is the key to the reader being able to understand the message.

Many of you will already have access to a personal computer and most of you will have access to one in the future. There are many software packages available which have graphics facilities. Many of them link with databases, report writers and spreadsheet facilities so that you can present data from them in a visual form. Not only are these very powerful facilities but they will enable you to draw professional graphics although you may not be an artist, and to present numerical data properly without the help of a statistician.

Varieties of presentation

There are a number of common graphs and charts which are regularly employed in business to assist the reader to visualise numbers and results. The ones which you are most likely to come across include:

    Bar charts
    Stacked bar charts
    Horizontal bar charts
    Pie charts
    Line graphs
    Pie bar comparison charts
    Bubble charts
    Pictograms

Bar charts

The most common statistical charts are bar charts, as shown in figure 9.

You do *not* need a degree in statistics to see what has happened to the firm's trading profit over this six year period. Imagine if the company had tried to use the caption "Six years' growth of profits!" Instead we can clearly see a growth from 1984–1987, a slight fall from the 1987 peak in 1988 and a substantial fall in 1989.

The very simplicity of the chart encourages you to ask questions such as:

    'What caused the growth from 1984 to 1987?
    'What was the reason for decline in profits after 1987?'

A bar chart is simply a series of blocks or bars in which each bar represents the total number of items being compared. The height of each bar is read from the vertical axis. It is often effective to draw the bars in three dimensions as this lengthens the visual impact.

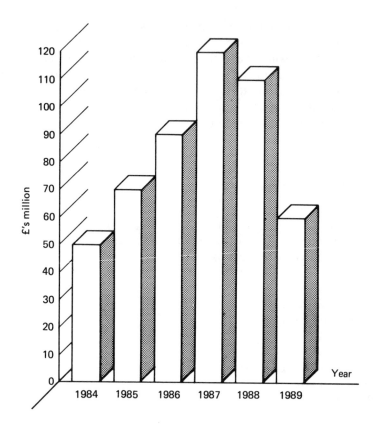

Figure 9   Bar chart showing trading profit, 1984–1989

When constructing a bar chart, it should be noted that the width of the bars or any gaps between them have no significance at all. The vertical scale must start at 0 so that the heights of each bar can be accurately compared.

Bar charts are very versatile and accurate. They can be represented vertically, horizontally or be combined with line graphs. They have strengths both in terms of accuracy and visual impact. As with every method of presentation, they have their limitations. They can only be used to compare a limited number of items and their impact is heightened when there are considerable differences between the items being compared.

Figures 10 and 11 show respectively two variations of the standard bar chart — the stacked bar chart and the horizontal bar chart.

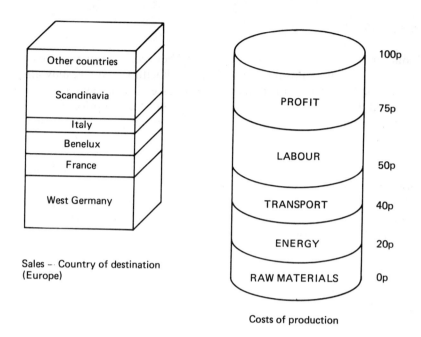

Figure 10   Stacked bar charts

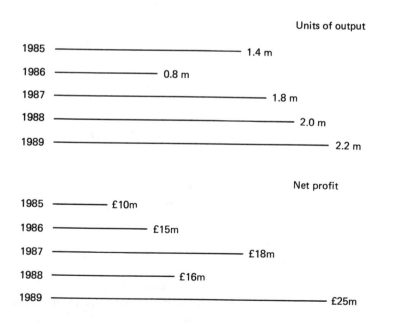

Figure 11   Horizontal bar charts

Line graphs

A line or *x/y* graph shows the relationship between two or more factors.

Figure 12 shows an example of a line graph with which you may already be familiar from the other units of your course. It is known as a *demand curve* and this graph shows the relationship between the price of a product and the amount of it which consumers demand at particular prices. It is easy to see that at high prices consumers will only want to consume small quantities, while a fall in price will mean that demand increases. The major advantage of the line graph is that it is easy to analyse the relationship between variables.

The graph is read as follows. If the price of product A is 60 pence per kilo then 10,000 are demanded, but if the price falls to 33 pence then the quantity demanded rises to 40,000 kilos.

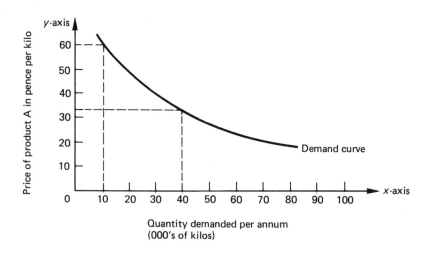

Figure 12   Demand curve for product A

The graph allows us to draw the conclusion and to answer questions such as:

'What is the consequence for demand of a 10 pence rise in price if the existing price is 20 pence?'
'How much of product A will be demanded at 50 pence?'
'If I want to sell 80,000 units what is the maximum price I can charge?'

Line graphs (see figure 13) are drawn up by constructing two scales:

(a) The vertical scale or *y*-axis. This must start from a point of origin and be divided into equal portions.

(b) The horizontal scale or *x*-axis. Again, this starts from a point of origin and is divided into equal portions. The division of the *x* and *y* scales do not have to be identical.

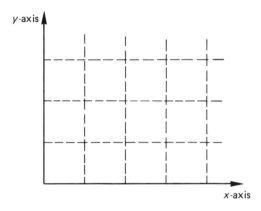

Figure 13

In order to construct a line graph, at least two sets of tabulated data are required. This must be data whose relationship we are concerned to discover. This data is plotted on the graph and a line is drawn to link the points. The use of graph paper makes accurate plotting possible — compare the tabulated results below and their plot in figure 14.

Price of *x* per kilo	Supply of *x*
10	10
20	20
30	30
40	50
50	70
60	90

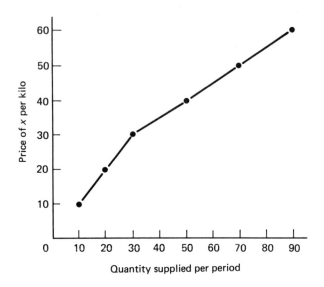

Figure 14   Supply curve

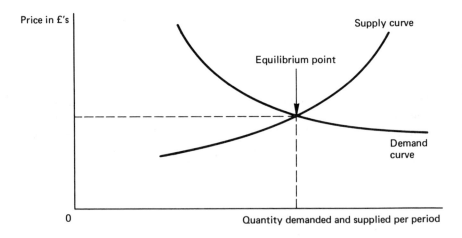

Figure 15   Combined demand and supply curves

It is possible to plot the relationship between a number of variables on the same graph. In the example in figure 15, we combine Demand and Supply graphs (figures 12 and 14) to produce a graph which can illustrate how price is determined in a competitive market.

The long-term price of the product is that where the differing interests of producers and customers converge. This is the point known as the equilibrium point. From this point the Market Price and the Quantity of the products demanded and supplied can be determined.

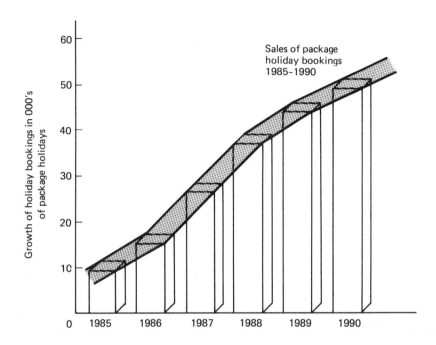

Figure 16   Combined bar and line graph

Combined bar and line graph

A combined bar and line graph (figure 16) simply combines two forms of representation. In our example, the relationship between each year's sales is shown by the bar chart but the line graph shows the trend over the period.

Pie charts

Another popular graph is the pie chart (see figure 17). It is usually employed for dealing with percentages where the whole circle represents 100% and the 'slices' or proportional segments show the fractional percentages. A very effective use is to show the proportion of costs in the manufacture of a product.

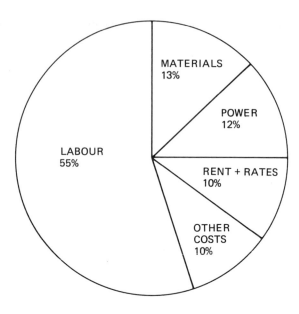

Figure 17   Costs of manufacturing

The whole circle, containing 360°, represents the total amount of whatever it is that is being divided up, in this case the total cost of manufacturing. In order to find the 'slices', each element is divided by the total and multiplied by 360. If the cost of Labour is £6600 and the total cost of manufacturing is £12,000, its slice is calculated as follows:

$$\frac{6600}{12000} \times 360° = 198°$$

The total costs of manufacturing and their respective slices are made up as follows:

Labour	6600	198°
Materials	1560	46.8°
Power	1440	43.2°
Rent & Rates	1200	36°
Other	1200	36°
Total	12000	360°

After calculating the angles for each, a protractor is required to draw these angles.

The usual convention, followed in this example, is to place the largest slice on the left and for the other slices to be drawn in descending order.

There are limitations to the use of pie charts. It is difficult for them to be drawn accurately and the human eye finds it difficult to detect small differences — in our example the slices representing 12% and 13% of the total. Pies can be confusing and cluttered if more than six or seven slices are displayed. They are useful only for a single set of data and cannot be used to compare two sets unless two pies each representing different totals are compared.

However, these criticisms are outweighed by the visual impact which pie charts have. They give a good general impression of the size of the figures involved in a clear visual form.

Bubble charts

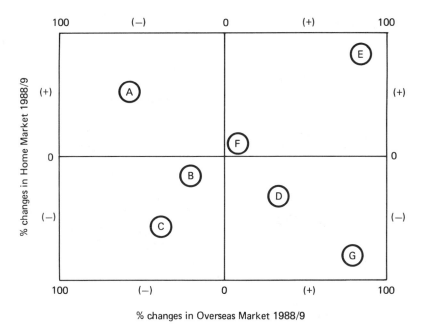

Figure 18   Bubble chart

Bubble charts are particularly useful when comparing the results of a number of different items. In figure 18, a company with seven products, code named A, B, C, D, E, F and G, is comparing their performance in the home and overseas markets:

Product E is the best performer in terms of growth, showing 80% + in both markets.

Product D is a growth performer in the overseas markets but its performance in the home market has declined from the previous year.

Activity: 'Bubble chart analysis'

Describe how products A, B, C, F and H have performed by analysing the bubble chart.

Pictograms

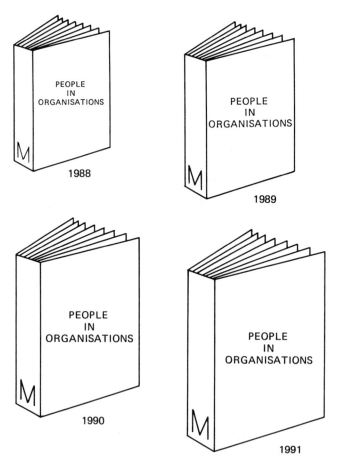

Figure 19   Pictogram

A pictogram (see figure 19) is often used for its eye-catching qualities. Its strength is that it is visual and easy to understand. In our example the size of the books represents the sales of the textbook. To compare one year with another, you merely compare the size of the pictures.

The drawback is obvious — accuracy and precision are missing. Even if we knew that, for example, the 1988 sales were 10,000 copies, what are the levels of sales for 1989 or 1990? The inability to convey accurate figures limits the use of pictograms except where we wish only to provide a general impression of a set of figures and where detail is not important.

CHAPTER 11

Giving a Talk

During your course you will be asked to give at least one talk. You may be asked to do the activity in this chapter of the book or a similar one devised by your lecturers. For many of you, giving a talk may be a nerve-wracking experience and yet you talk to people quite naturally every day of your life. You need to ask yourself what is so different when it comes to talking to an audience? The difference is the stress you experience when you have to stand up and address other people.

When you give a talk you become the focus of attention. The audience will listen carefully to what you have to say. You can be the centre of attention in a conversation but then the focus changes as new participants enter the dialogue. In conversation, people do not fix their eyes on you and make notes: they are informal and natural, while talks are set piece, formal occasions.

With a talk, the topic is specified in advance and you will be expected to keep to your brief. In conversation, we deviate as and when we like. You may start talking about a particular subject and finish discussing something very different. There is no length to a discussion, unlike a talk where speakers are given a specific time for delivery.

Talks are then a special and different activity, requiring practice to master. Initially, they are stressful but that is not a reason to avoid them. There is a challenge in doing something that is difficult and a sense of achievement when it is finished, especially when the audience applauds.

Preparing for a talk

The audience

When giving a talk or making a speech you must be aware of whom you are going to talk to. Many talks fail because speakers talk down or over the heads of their audience. The age, sex, background and expertise of the audience are all important factors for consideration. You need to remember that you can be very technical when talking to experts but that the same illuminating technicalities will bewilder an audience comprising only lay people. The size of the audience is also an important factor to keep in mind. It is possible to be informal and adopt a conversational style with a small audience, but the larger the audience the more formal your talk needs to be

You need to keep your audience in mind when you are preparing for your talk. The type of audience you are addressing will affect what you will say and how you say it.

The content and structure

You must spend time preparing the content of your talk. You must be clear what you are talking about and you must have marshalled all the necessary facts and information. After doing this, you need to structure your material in such a way that the audience will be able to follow the arguments and the drift of your thinking. You will need an introduction which states clearly what you are talking about and why. This is called 'flagging' and it signals to your audience what the talk will be about. The way you start is most important because if you lose your audience at the beginning you will find it difficult to win back their attention. Try to find a vivid illustration of your theme to start off your talk. This will help to stimulate the audience's interest in what you are going to say.

It will be helpful to make notes for your talk but do avoid reading them. You cannot read and make eye contact with the audience. You must look at your audience when talking to them. What you need to do is to rehearse your talk so that the final delivery can be fluent and easy. Always visualise your audience when practising, as this will help you in choosing the right tone for your voice. Do not learn your lines, as this can make the talk rather stilted unless you are a competent actor. You must not be afraid of thinking on your feet and adding good ideas that occur to you as you speak.

Writing a plan

While you must not read a speech, you should make notes. These are aids to enable you to keep to your theme and they provide a logical consistency to the talk. The type of notes you make are personal but the important point is that you can follow them with only a glance. Some speakers prefer a series of underlined headings, others divide the page in two and put the headings on the left and supporting information on the right. A popular method is to use post cards. They can be held in the hand. The usual method is to write each main point and supporting information on a single card. Because they are small they do not give the audience the impression that you are reading from notes which does happen if your notes are on A4 size paper.

Visual aids

The use of visual aids can be helpful to your talk but they are an *aid* and should not substitute for what you intend to say. Do not use visual aids for the sake of using them and do not use them as a defence to hide behind if you are nervous. If you decide to use them, make certain that they are clear, well-presented and can be read by your audience. Poorly produced visual aids are worse than no aids at all.

The type of aid you can use will vary depending on your subject, but you can think about using:

- Notes written on a transparency and projected on to a screen by an overhead projector.
- Notes previously written on a flip chart pad.
- Handout notes. You should be careful how you use them because the audience may read these rather than listen to you.
- Slides projected by a slide projector. These can be very effective if your talk requires a high degree of visual impact. Make certain that your slides are good ones as they will be the focus of the talk.
- Video films. These substitute for a talk and should be used sparingly. People are very used to watching television for entertainment and not for information.
- Chalk board notes. If you use this method, make certain that you write them on the board before the talk and that your writing is legible. While this method is suitable for teaching, it is not a good one for business presentations. Overhead projectors provide more flexibility and masking techniques allow you to highlight areas which you want audiences to concentrate on.
- Models, charts and other devices. If you are talking about marketing pot plants, then some of the sample plants will help to draw your audience's attention to the subject.

The message about using visual aids is to use what is appropriate to the talk and do not let the technique dominate the context. In this area, the message is more important than the medium of communication.

Activity: 'A talk'

You are requested to give a talk to the members of your group on a topic of your choice. The only stipulation is that the topic must have some relationship to business activity or current affairs. You will be required to talk for about 15 minutes. If it assists your talk, you can use visual or other aids to illustrate it. You can bring notes with you for the talk but you should avoid reading them to your audience.

At the end of your talk you will be expected to answer any questions which the audience may have to ask.

You will be assessed on your ability to:

- Present an interesting, lively, and well-structured talk on your chosen topic. The information should be clearly presented and it should be plain to the audience: what the topic is; why you have chosen it; what view you take on the matter; and why you have arrived at any particular conclusions.
- Effectively use notes, and other aids, when giving your talk.
- Answer questions from the audience effectively.

CHAPTER 12

Communicating by Computer

The first commercial computer was introduced by the Sperry company in 1951. The original computers were vast affairs in large metal cabinets, housed in carefully regulated and air-conditioned environments. Nowadays, the small desk top personal computers, with which you are familiar, are more flexible and powerful.

The initial computer revolution was particularly evident on the financial side of businesses — the calculation of the payroll, the billing of customers and stock control — the early computers were successful at handling large amounts of data and crunching numbers. Today, business activity has been revolutionised by the application of computer technology. The local supermarket runs its checkout by optical character recognition of the bar codes printed on grocery items. The garage has computerised control of its pumps, and a business without computers in its accounts office and word processing equipment for its secretaries is considered antiquated. Businesses have to handle, store, process, retrieve and communicate vast amounts of information and, for this reason, an understanding of computer techniques and applications are essential aspects of business education.

Computers were once the province of the data processing department and, although central services are still of crucial importance, much of the mystery of computing has vanished as desk top computers have become an easily accessible tool.

Computers are used to provide databases to store and sort information; as word processors for the easy and effective production of documents; for spreadsheet operations which provide a means of displaying and manipulating financial and other numerical data; and for communicating via electronic mail both within and without the organisation. The latter function is becoming increasingly important in modern offices. Personal computers are being networked together or linked to minis and mainframes to provide communications networks which have fast and effective means of transmitting information. Computers are linked to the telephone network via modems, and messages can be carried world wide by satellite or through fibre optic cables.

> *Computers are important for all of us as they have changed the way we work and the way in which we communicate with each other.*

Business and office communications have been changed and are being changed by the impact of new technology. Office communications are being tailored to the demands of the computer. Computers are very flexible in the way they handle data and text, but the demands of screen layout and printer technology affect the way in which people compose their business communications. Spelling-checkers on word processor software may in time come to dominate and dictate the spelling of words rather than conventional dictionaries.

An obvious impact of the computer is in the way in which text is composed in the office. At one time the pen was the main instrument for this, followed by shorthand dictation. The use of audio equipment added a third technology but it was assumed, until comparatively recently, that the QWERTY keyboard was the province of the secretary and the typist. A manager would not have dreamed of typing and would have seen it as a demeaning activity.

Nowadays, typewriting has been retitled 'keyboarding' and the use of the computer keyboard is an essential managerial skill. It is for this reason that keyboarding is a key skill area on your course as it provides you with access to computing and computing power. Keyboarding may be a skill with a rather limited life as there are many other ways of inputing data, such as the mouse and touch screens. Eventually, voice recognition will mean that a person will be able to dictate directly to a computer and this will open up a new range of fascinating oral communication skills.

The language of computing

All technologies and working methods have their own language and jargon. Computers are a special case of this because their influence is so all-embracing that computer language has become an element in everyday speech. There are some people who wish to resist this change. They dislike the American spelling of 'program', and decry such terms as 'booting up', 'debug' and 'hands-on' as ugly slang. We have made the point elsewhere in this book that our language is living and changing. If a word or phrase is in ordinary use and is seen to perform a function, then it is a legitimate part of

English. We all take for granted the language of other twentieth century technologies like that of the motor car, the popular music industry, electricity, nuclear physics, space exploration and aviation. The technicalities of computing fall into the same category. To communicate about technical matters makes a special vocabulary necessary.

Computing has a large number of essentially transitory and fashionable terms, although other words will undoubtedly become permanent features of everyday speech. 'Software' and 'hardware' are good examples of computer technology which aids the understanding and appreciation of the technology.

An appreciation of computer terminology is important in business. A knowledge of the language is the key to opening the doors on any subject. Once you know the language you can talk to the computer professionals, read the technical press and ask the right questions. Knowing what to ask and what you are looking for enables you to make sensible choices about computing and not to waste time on applications which are irrelevant to you and your needs.

One important point to note is that computer terminology is an international language and is, therefore, an easy means of communicating with other business users worldwide.

Some computer essentials

This book is *not* intended to be a handbook on computing. There are plenty of useful books on this topic, some of which are listed in the Bibliography at the end of this book. What we do aim to do is to highlight some of the areas of computing and information technology which will be of concern to you as workers within organisations.

Most offices have or will soon have a range of personal computers and you should be familiar with the essentials of the hardware of PCs and the main varieties of software which can operate on them.

Hardware and software

Computer *hardware* (see figure 20) is the actual equipment, whether it is the visual display unit, the keyboard, disc drives or the printer. *Software* is a term which refers to the programs which provide the instructions to the computer.

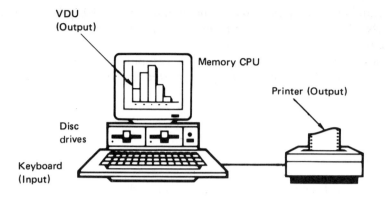

VDU
(Output)

Memory CPU

Printer (Output)

Disc
drives

Keyboard
(Input)

Figure 20   Hardware

Input devices

The most common means of inputing data into a computer is via a keyboard. This consists of a QWERTY keyboard, familiar from typewriters, together with a range of function keys. Unfortunately, except for the QWERTY element, layouts vary considerably, although there is some standardisation among certain IBM and compatible machines.

Other means of inputing data include the mouse. This is a small box on a roller ball which is moved around a desk top. The position of the mouse affects the appropriate menus and buttons on top of the mouse are flicked to give commands to the program. It can be used in conjunction with the keyboard.

Touch screens are also used with menu-driven software to give commands. The operator simply touches the screen at the appropriate part of the menu and the instruction is given. Neither the mouse nor the touch screen have the flexibility of the keyboard; their advantage is that they require less skill to operate them.

Output devices

Text or data is displayed to the operator on a visual display unit. The monitors can either be colour or two tone — green on black, white on black, black on yellow, etc. It is becoming usual for programs to be written so that the information on the screen is WYSIWYG — 'What you see is what you get'. This means that the hard copy from the printer will be very similar to the information displayed on the screen.

Printers provide hard copy for the operator and this is produced via dot matrix, daisy wheel or laser technology. Printers are available for continuous feed paper or for one-off copies.

Another form of output occurs where computers are networked to each other so that the input of one is outputted on the screen or printer of another user.

The Central Processing Unit

The Central Processing Unit (CPU) contains the various functional parts which enable a computer to operate. For all practical purposes, we can consider this aspect as a 'black box' and not concern ourselves with its operation. Knowing that it works when we switch the machine on is sufficient for our purposes. One essential piece of information is the amount of memory capacity a particular machine has. Most business PCs have memories of 256K, 512K or 640K, although the more expensive hard disc versions provide a much greater storage capacity. The size of the memory is important only because certain business programs require a considerable memory capacity. You need to match memory carefully to software requirements.

Disc drives

For business applications there are two types of discs available for PCs — the fixed or hard disc, often known as Winchester discs, and floppy discs. The former can normally hold up to 20 megabytes of data. The advantage of hard discs is that they store not only data but also the programs required for a particular job. For large databases or applications such as integrated accounts packages, they represent the best solution as they avoid the constant changing of discs which would occur if the system were to run on floppy discs.

Floppy discs represent a cheaper system of loading programs and storing data than hard discs. But they store less information. Their other advantage is that they can be unloaded and transferred to other machines. In small businesses with intermittent use of computers they represent an ideal solution. Originally, floppy discs were of 8-inch format, but the industry standard is now the $5\frac{1}{4}$-inch disc with $3\frac{1}{2}$-inch and 3-inch discs gaining in popularity. The discs themselves are relatively cheap and about 60 pages of text can be stored on a typical double-density $5\frac{1}{4}$-inch disc.

Software

In the early days of computing, all software had to be specially written for every use made of a computer. Today, most computing is carried out using commercially produced applications programs. The vast majority of computer users cannot and have no need to write programs. What they require is an understanding of what they want to be able to do and a knowledge of what software is commercially available to them. Custom-built programs are, of course, written every day but they are only undertaken for special tasks or when there is no satisfactory commercial product. It is usually large organisations that have programs specially written for them. In most businesses, especially those that rely on personal computers, the software is invariably commercially available packages.

The three most common types of package for business use are:

SPREADSHEETS
DATABASES
WORD PROCESSORS

Spreadsheets

The spreadsheet is derived from manual accounting systems and is a powerful business tool as it allows for the processing of a very large quantity of numerical information.

The computer spreadsheet (see figure 21) consists of a number of compartments, sometimes called 'cells'. They are arranged into horizontal rows and vertical columns. The spreadsheet is a matrix of cells and into each can be put numbers, formulas, titles and instructions. Some spreadsheets have as many as 250 columns width and are over 8000 rows deep. With these large spreadsheets, the computer screen shows only a section of what can be thought of as a giant sheet of continuous stationery.

	1987	1988	1989	1990	1991
Guildford	2415	2450	2693	2489	2340
Godalming	4316	4520	4810	4936	5306
Haslemere	7832	6521	6318	6480	7232
Alton	459	630	751	831	932
Redhill	8730	8752	8763	8832	8959
	23 752	22 873	23 335	25 568	24 769

Figure 21   A spreadsheet

Columns and rows can be added, subtracted and analysed mathematically in a variety of ways. Calculations which would take many hours manually can be performed instantly. This means that sophisticated 'What if' analysis can be made. A company could, for example, look at its projected raw material costs and ask 'what if the exchange rate for the £ changes?', 'what if interest rates rise or fall by so much?', and so on.

Spreadsheets were originally used in business as an accounting tool to create balance sheets, plan budgets, cash flow forecasts and forward financial plans. They are now used for any planning purpose which requires the analysis of figures. Applications include human resource forecasting, calculating percentages and costing projects.

The most sophisticated packages have graphics facilities to enable graphics and bar charts to be constructed from the numerical data. There are a large number of spreadsheets on the market and some of the more popular include:

Lotus 1–2–3
SuperCalc 2 and SuperCalc 3
Microsoft Multiplan

Databases

Like spreadsheets, databases are not limited to computers. Any organised system of information constitutes a database and this includes libraries, telephone directories, reference books, filing cabinets and address books. Any database, whether it is computerised or not, contains information which is arranged according to pre-determined rules. That is to say, information may be arranged alphabetically, according to a geographical location or according to some other function. The reason for this flexibility is to make it easy to find the entry you require provided you know how to use the classification system.

In computing, the term 'database' is used to describe virtually any system which holds records or information. However, it is useful to distinguish between systems which merely hold information and those which organise and control the data held in them.

The uses of databases are endless. You could keep menus, telephone directories, staff lists, customer records, product information and personnel records on them. The advantage that databases have over manual filing systems is the ability to upgrade the same information held in many files at the same time. For example, if we take a personnel records system, a female employee who marries and changes her name will require to have her file updated. But her name may appear a number of times in various files. Once the change has been entered, then all the entries will have been updated. Furthermore, the information stored in the computer database, unlike that in a conventional one, such as a telephone directory, can be manipulated in a variety of ways. As well as providing appropriate telephone numbers, a computerised database incorporating the information contained in a telephone directory could tell us the number of people with double-barrelled names, or the number of dentists living in a particular area, or it could print out all those with the surname of, say, Jones.

Popular databases include

Ashton-Tate's dBase III
Compsoft's Delta 4

Data Protection Act

Databases are one of the most important uses of computers. Records of all types are kept on a computer and are easily accessed. In recent years, concern has been expressed about the use, or rather the misuse, which this vast amount of information could be put to. For this reason there is now legislation which covers the keeping of computerised records. *The Data Protection Act 1984* demands that anyone who holds or controls computerised data of a personal nature must register it with the Data Protection Registrar. Individuals have important rights of access to their records. It is an offence under the Act to obtain, process or disclose data without registering. The only exceptions are data kept for domestic, family or recreational purposes. This means that even a local parish church with a list of parishioners on a computerised database must register under the Act.

Word processors

Word processing can be carried out either by computers which are dedicated to the task or by purchasing a software package for a PC. Word processing allows for text to be manipulated on a screen. Among other applications it provides:

- A filing system for text.
- A means of merging names and addresses.
- A text-editing facility.
- A spelling-check facility.
- A mail-merging facility (a means of sending personalised standard letters by merging a list of addresses from a database with a standard form letter).

Word processors are more than just sophisticated typewriters, although many electronic typewriters do have limited memories and can be upgraded and linked to screens to give them word processing capabilities. In order to make the best use of word processing it is useful to know where it has advantages over conventional typewriters. The following specialist uses are particularly associated with word processors:

- Word processors can be used as electronic filing systems.
- Word processors are very useful report compilers, especially where there is a need to merge and edit text.
- Word processors are useful marketing aids, especially for the production of personalised standard letters. Mail-merge facilities allow for the merging of names and addresses with standard letter formats.
- Authorship can be improved because word processing allows for constant revision without the need to retype whole documents or significant sectors of them.
- There are improved opportunities for checking and proof reading. Spelling and grammar checks can take place in this process.

There is a considerable variety of equipment and packages available to business users. The essential elements to bear in mind when choosing a system are:

- The user friendliness of the system.
- The market share of the package. This will provide a guide to the level of support which the manufacturers provide for it and the level of training which will be available. A popular system will have a great deal more support for the individual user.
- The training and support which is available for the package.

Popular word processing software includes:

Micropro's	WordStar
	WordStar 2000
Ashton-Tate's	Multimate
IBM's	Display Write IV
Microsoft's	Word

Activity: 'Word processing'

All word processing systems have disadvantages as well as strengths. Choose two systems and spend a little time on a computer becoming familiar with their main features. You could produce two assignments, each using a different system. From your experience of using each system, assess the advantages of each system and suggest improvements which you would like the manufacturers to make to their product.

Integrated software

Packages have been designed to end the shuffling of floppy discs by integrating databases, word processing and spreadsheets into a single package. They usually have additional graphics and communications facilities. The size of the memory on the PC needs to be large and a RAM memory of 640K is usually necessary to run them. The Lotus Symphony, Ashton-Tate's Framework and Psion Systems' Xchange are popular examples of such software. They are very powerful and flexible tools but demand a considerable investment in time for the user to become familiar with them.

Electronic communications

Electronic mail is the name given to sending messages electronically via a computer network or around the world using telephone links. The advantages of electronic mail over more traditional communication forms are considerable. The production of a message, say a memo, can be produced by the author and sent virtually instantaneously to any number of subscribers linked to the system.

Consider the usual 'system' for sending office memos:

1. Manager writes or dictates (either verbally or to a dictating machine) the memo.
2. Secretary types the memo.
3. Secretary returns typed memo for manager to proof read and for signature.
4. Manager passes completed memo to the secretary.
5. Secretary copies memo on a photocopying machine.
6. Secretary distributes memo, either by putting it in a pigeon hole or directly into recipients' in-tray.
7. Secretary files the original of the memo.

With electronic mail the whole system is simplified:

1. Manager types the memo directly on to the screen of his or her PC, which is linked to other terminals in the network. Proof reading and editing are carried out at this stage.

2. A few key strokes send the memo instantly to the recipient's electronic mail box. Another key stroke ensures that the memo is stored in the computer's memory.

Electronic mail can be accessed by an employee who is out of the office or who is in another part of the building. In order to read a paper memo, the recipients must physically return to their desks or pigeon holes. With electronic mail, the electronic mail box can be accessed from any other terminal in the network. Additionally, it is possible to access messages from a distance, even on the other side of the world with a PC linked to the telephone system via a modem. The fact that many PCs are portable means that memos or messages can be read in telephone booths in, say, airport lounges.

Networking computers

Many organisations purchase stand-alone PCs and then find that the file of one user is frequently required by another user. This is not a problem as discs can easily be copied and transferred to another machine. But it assumes that one user knows what another has on disc. There is an easier and simpler way of sharing data, and that is to *network* the machines so that all the data in the system can be easily shared and accessed by all the users. The installation in an office environment is known as a *Local Area Network* or *LAN*.

What do networks offer?

Shared resources — this is the most important reason for establishing a network. It allows a number of users to access central resources such as a central database, electronic devices, printers, etc. This allows the collection of PCs which make up the network to have some of the facilities found on mainframes. The PCs are closely integrated and this in turn means that office routines have to be more closely integrated. Doing this can reduce duplication and cost.

Communications — networks provide easy access to external electronic mail systems such as British Telecom Gold, or provide the organisation with its own internal communications system. Simply, it is easy to send messages around the system.

Analysis of LANs

Strengths

Flexibility — the installation of a LAN increases the number of users, the number of add-ons and the number of applications which the system can be put to

Weaknesses

Cost — networks are expensive to cable and to install

Reliability — LANs have to be properly managed and to have a technical backup if they are to provide a good service

Compatibility — it is important that all the hardware and software in the system is compatible. Users can only use compatible hardware and software

Opportunities

Communications — LANs provide increased communications facilities via electronic mail

Shared resources — users can share the data and the software available on the LAN

Threats

Organisation — users of PCs in LANs lose their freedom to operate as they like. They must use the PC and the software which are centrally purchased and supplied. The freedom provided by the PC over the mainframe user is forfeited

Types of networks

Star networks

This is the simplest form of network. The Terminals are connected to a central mainframe or minicomputer. This system may use 'dumb' terminals — that is, monitors which do not have their own central processing facility and which only display information from the mainframe. The star

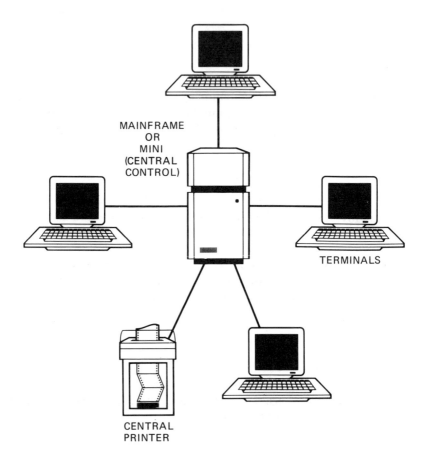

network relies on the central control to decide on which station to divert data. Individual stations can only communicate via the central control. Star networks often use dedicated cabling which means that bottlenecks can be eliminated and faults can be more easily diagnosed.

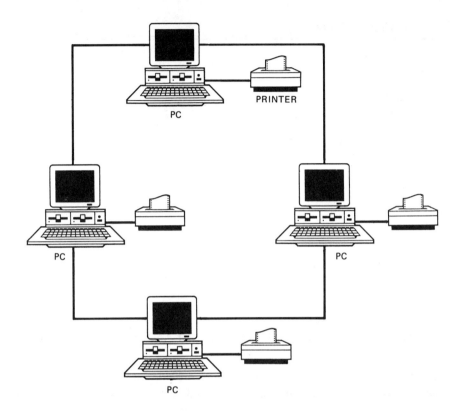

Ring networks

Ring networks allow for each free-standing PC to be linked to a continuous path around the system. The computers can be used as stand-alone micros, as each has its own disc drives and printer. The benefit is that each machine can communicate with every other machine in the LAN. It allows for the traffic to be easily spread throughout the system.

A variant is known as the *token ring network* or *token passing network*. In this system, stations are given turns at using the network. Only when the token is held by an individual station can a transmission be sent.

Non-discriminatory Language

As an introduction to the topic of non-discriminatory language we want you to consider the following job titles:

SENIOR SALESMAN
CHAIRMAN OF THE MANPOWER PLANNING COMMITTEE

What do these titles tell us? Firstly, they provide information about two functional roles common in business — that is, being a senior member of the salesforce and the chairing of a committee planning the use of human resources. The second thing which these titles tell us is rather more subtle, and it is that the organisation would normally expect these roles to be filled by men.

In recent years, many observers have started to pay attention to the way in which language can reinforce the disadvantage which various groups experience. For example, advertisements such as those which consistently use business*man* as the synonym for people in business seek to remind women that in many areas of commercial life it is still a man's world. Discriminatory language has the effect of demotivating those discriminated against by informing them that it is others in society who are more important and have a natural right to fill certain positions. The use of language can and does disadvantage women and members of ethnic minority groups. The latter are usually discriminated against by overt racist language which denigrates a person's colour and ethnic background. Discrimination against women is of a different type, for whereas racial discrimination comes from slang usage, sexual discrimination is present in the formal structure of our language.

Many authors writing in the third person use 'he' and 'his', even when the references include or refer to women. Other examples of discrimination are to be found in role titles such as foreman or tradesman widely used in business and elsewhere which imply that the positions are normally (and rightly?) filled by men.

It is often argued that it is very difficult to write without making constant use of masculine pronouns or words which have a masculine connotation. We hope that by employing non-discriminatory usage in this book we have shown that it is possible and easy to adopt another style. Another argument commonly used to defend the *status quo* is that sexist titles are 'correct' and that 'everybody knows' that when they write 'he' they also mean 'she'. This is the view which also says that certain forms of language 'are correct'. But if we stop to think, we realise that language is constantly changing and what is correct is only so because it is accepted as such. What defenders of titles such as 'chairman' are doing is defending male superiority and not the English language.

The reason for being aware of sexism in language is that it biases experience constantly towards the male sex and gives little or no prominence to the role of women in society. We find organisations who employ both men and women talking about exercises in *man*power planning, discussing the performance of their sales*men* not their salesforce, and having meetings chaired by chair*men*. The constant use of 'he' when talking and writing about managers gives many women and girls the impression that it is an uphill struggle if they want a career in a leadership position. Equal opportunities demands that we need to employ a language which is not biased in favour of any particular group. In the table that follows we provide a guide to avoiding discriminatory language.

Common discriminatory words	*Non-discriminatory alternatives*
Manpower	Personnel, Human resources
Housewife	Homemaker
Mankind	Human beings, Human species
Workman	Worker
Manmade	Human creation
Man of letters	Writer, Author
Man-in-the-street⎫ Commonman ⎬	⎧Common people, Ordinary ⎩Folk, People
Everyman	Everyone
Manhours	Hours of work
Nightwatchman	Guard, Security guard
Chairman	Chair, Chairperson
Businessman	Businessperson
Craftsman	Craftsperson, Artisan
Salesman/Salesgirl	Salesperson
Repairman	Repairer
Fireman	Firefighter
Foreman	Supervisor
Cameraman	Camera operator

Yes-man	Crawler, sycophant
Weatherman	Weatherforecaster
To man (verb)	To staff, serve, work, people,
as in 'to man the ship',	run, operate
'to man the barricades', or	So instead of 'the telephone
'man the office'	must be manned at all times'
	we could write it in a non-
	discriminatory way as 'the tele-
	phone must be *staffed* at all
	times'

As well as titles which imply male ownership there are, of course, a number of titles which refer to roles usually filled by females. Examples are Housewife, Charlady, Tealady, Salesgirl, Girl Friday, Waitress and Chambermaid. They are usually low status roles, whereas the roles given the masculine gender are usually high status, such as Businessman. There are occasional exceptions to this such as 'Office boy', but in the main the roles specifying the female gender refer to low and often subservient roles. We need to avoid the use of low status female gender role terms with the same care that we take to avoid male gender titles.

Activity: 'Alternative titles'

Below are some common sexist titles. You should find suitable non-sexist alternatives to them.

Ambulanceman	Girl Friday	Office Boy
Draughtsman	Airline stewardess	Founding-fathers
Fisherman	Statesman	Tradesman
Doorman	Tea lady	Policeman
Sportsman	Charlady	Maid
Milkman		Layman

There are problems and dilemmas in using non-discriminatory language. Traditionally, the word 'black' has had a meaning as 'dishonourable' and 'evil' and so terms like 'blacking', 'blackleg', 'blackspot', 'blackmarket', 'blackguard' and 'blackmail' refer to antisocial behaviour. The use of 'black' to describe unscrupulous or villainous behaviour may be repugnant to many members of ethnic minority communities in Britain and we should be careful about their use. There are plenty of acceptable alternatives, such as 'boycott' for 'blacking', 'extortion' for 'blackmail', 'danger area' for 'blackspot'.

'Managers'

Casey Miller and Kate Swift in their book on sexist language make the point that there are a number of words with the prefix 'man' which have nothing to do with the male gender. Such words as *manager*, *manipulate*, *manuscript*, and *manufacture* derive from the Latin word *manus* 'the hand'. They argue, sensibly, that for this reason it would be ridiculous to find alternatives for the syllable 'man' in these words.

SECTION III

ORGANISATIONS

CHAPTER 14

The Structure of Organisations

Anyone joining an organisation needs to find out quickly how the organisation is structured and how it works. If you think back to joining the College, you will realise how important this was to you. You needed to know what group you were in, who was in charge of that group, what the rules of attendance and work were, what was expected of you and by what criteria your work was going to be measured. The list, we suspect, probably seemed endless. The first few days in any organisation are all about issues like these. Many organisations, College included, realise this and organise induction sessions for their new members to familiarise themselves with the basic characteristics of the organisation.

As a member of an organisation yourself, you will have come to realise how complex and varied they are. You will also have made a discovery that what seems to you to be the main features or focus may be seen differently by other people with whom you come in contact. What seems to you to be a very minor regulation may appear to be a major infringement of liberty to another. What seems well organised to you is a source of frustration to others. Some people like to have a clear set of rules to live and to work by, while others condemn these same rules as 'bureaucratic', restrictive and stifling. Another aspect of organisations which you might have discovered is that organisations are constantly changing. Ask someone who left your course and College some years ago. You will find that their recollections are different from the way the College is now. Organisations are in a constant state of flux caused by such things as changes in personnel, changes in technology and changes in the environment in which they operate (see figure 22).

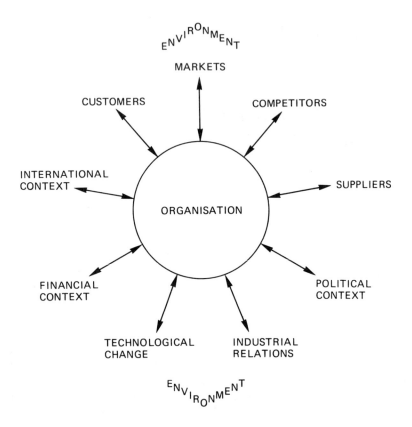

Figure 22   The organisation in its environment

How are organisations structured?

'Form follows function' is a phrase which is often used when discussing organisational structures. It means that the design of the structure — the form — has to be led by the function which has to be performed if the organisation is to be successful. For this reason no two organisations have the same structure. An engineering plant and an advertising agency are different and this difference will be reflected in their organisational design.

Nevertheless, there are common features in organisational structures and it is helpful to analyse some of the most typical features.

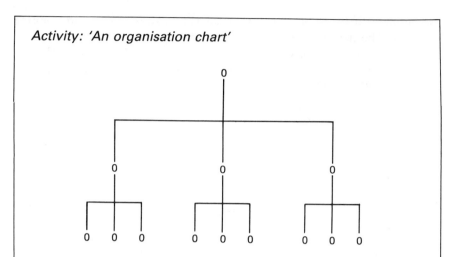

Activity: 'An organisation chart'

What characteristics of hierarchical structures can you deduce from studying the chart? (You ought to be able to deduce at least five. The answers are given on page 111, but to start you off: how many management tiers does this organisation have?)

Organisational design

Different organisations have different structures. The design of an organisation depends on the goals it is pursuing, its size, its market, the environment in which it operates and the technology it is employing. The way in which an organisation is structured depends upon the way its members feel it will best survive in the world.

There are numbers of ways in which organisations can be structured.

Geographically based organisations

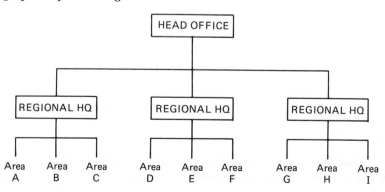

Geographically based organisations such as retail businesses readily spring to mind. The major units of say Marks and Spencer, or Boots are their High Street stores. Banks and Building Societies also have geographically based structures. Manufacturing companies with dispersed plants will follow a similar pattern.

Market based organisations

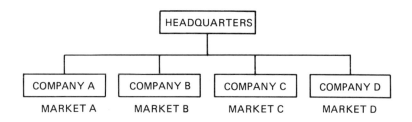

Some organisations are planned to conform to the structure of their markets. In some cases this provides a variation on the geographically based structure. But it may be that the company is producing a range of products and has set up separate units or subsidiaries to exploit each product market.

Functionally based organisations

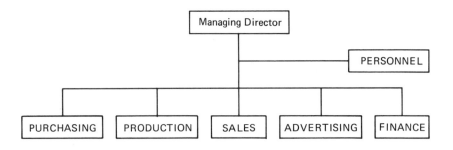

In this structure the organisation is designed around the different *functions* required to make and sell its product or service.

Product based organisations

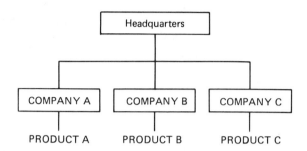

In this structure the organisation is designed according to the product which is being manufactured. Each company/unit will have its own manufacturing, accounting, sales and purchasing functions.

Matrix organisations

The matrix structure has become popular in recent years with project based organisations and with many educational establishments. Its critics argue that it is complex and confusing and requires people to spend a lot of their time attending meetings. Its supporters make the point that it breaks down rigid hierarchies and allows for greater participation in the decision-making process.

A matrix structure

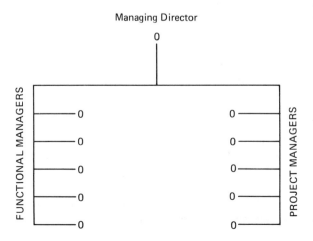

In a typical matrix there are *two* hierarchies — in this case there are Functional Managers who have staff and resources but no work, and Project Managers who control the work but have no staff and resources of their own. The Functional Managers' job is to provide the staffing and the resourcing for the projects which the organisation is undertaking. It is their job to see that all the resources in their area of responsibility are suitable for the projects being undertaken.

Project Managers are freed from direct responsibility for staff so they can give their attention to the effective management of their project. They call upon the resources provided by the Functional Managers.

Each staff member reports to two bosses — his or her Project Manager and his or her specialist manager. This aspect can cause some confusion. The fundamental organisational principle — unity of command — is broken. It is a tenet of most organisations that people only have one direct manager. In order to avoid the confusion which could be caused if employees were given two divergent sets of goals to pursue, matrix management involves a complex committee system and relies on good and regular internal communications.

Activity: 'College structure'

On what basis is your College organised? Is it

- Customer/client based
- Functionally based
- Geographically based
- Market based
- Product/service based
- A matrix organisation

You should discuss why you have come to your particular conclusions about its form of organisation.

Response to technological change — mechanistic and organic structures

The distinction between two models of organisation structure — mechanistic and organic — derives from the work of T. Burns and E. M. Stalker in their book *The Management of Innovation* (1966). Their ideas grew out of research carried out in the electronics industry where companies face high rates of technological change.

Two basic forms of organisation were found to operate. One they describe as mechanistic, the other as organic.

The mechanistic structures were machine like. They were functionally divided with defined chains of command. That is to say, there was someone with the responsibility for each operation accountable to 'somebody at the top'. There was a precise definition of task and job. Interaction and communication mainly followed vertical lines — and was mainly top downwards. Operators did what they did because of orders coming from the top.

The other form of organisation was dubbed 'organic'. In these organisations, jobs had lost much of their formal definition and there was a constant redefinition of tasks. Because of this, responsibilities and functions were redefined through interactions with others while participating in common tasks. Communications were lateral as well as vertical.

Burns and Stalker found that organic structures were better able to respond to change than mechanistic ones. The 'network structure' of control, authority and communications provided a greater commitment on the part of the workforce and made it better able to respond to change.

Does this mean that defining jobs and structures is a mistake? There is plenty of work from other managerial researchers to contradict it. Elliot Jacques and Wilfred Brown, in their longitudinal studies associated with the Glazier Metals Company, found that individuals have a felt need to have their role and status clearly defined in ways that are acceptable to them and their colleagues. Ambiguities as to roles can lead to stress and frustration. The Glazier Metals work demonstrated the importance of channels for participation and communication but seems to dispute the informal and evolutionary structures associated with organic organisations.

The structure of organisations largely depends upon functions. Entrepreneurial organisations in highly competitive and technologically fast changing environments need first and foremost to respond to change and to innovate. For them, speed of action in decision-making and for innovation is all important. Other organisations have different goals — institutions such as banks have to put accountability, reliability and security high on their list of priorities. For them it is important to pinpoint responsibilities and to define functions carefully. Accountability of this type favours mechanistic structures.

Answers to 'organisation chart' activity on page 107

- There are two tiers of management.
- The organisation is a hierarchy, with a formal chain of command.
- The organisation is divided into three (these could be geographical divisions — say 3 shops, or functional divisions, which could be production, accounts and sales — or product based divisions).

- The organisation employs 13 employees, four of whom occupy management roles.
- There is one overall 'boss' — who might be titled Managing Director, Chief Executive, President, Principal, etc.
- The span of control for each of the 4 Managers is 3 employees.
- There is 'unity of command' which is to say that each member of the organisation only has one direct supervisor.
- It can be assumed that the degree of power and authority of each role holder increases towards the apex of the hierarchy.
- Each manager is accountable for the work of his or her sections, departments, shops or whatever name is given to each division of the organisation.

Formal and informal organisations

Much organisational theory concentrates upon the *formal* structure of organisations. That is to say upon the documented and officially described features of the organisation. The formal structure is the structure of the organisation charts which we have drawn up in this chapter. But organisation charts only give us the bare bones of the organisation's structure and we should not be carried away with the idea that official descriptions tell us all.

It might be useful to think of an organisation chart as a kind of London Underground map. As you are probably aware, the *actual* network of lines and stations beneath London's streets does *not* conform to the neat, straight lines with regularly spaced stations depicted on the map. The lines weave and turn and the stations are not regularly placed. The map is drawn to help the traveller, not to be an accurate reflection of reality. Similarly, the organisation chart is an idealised guide.

> Some people argue that the INFORMAL ORGANISATION describes what really goes on in an organisation whereas the FORMAL ORGANISATION describes what ought to happen.

To understand the workings of an organisation we need to impose the structure of human relationships on top of the formal structure. The informal structure is the structure as it actually operates rather than the way it ought to operate. If we look at the two charts in figures 23 and 24, we can see how they intermesh. Figure 23 shows a typical formal structure embodied in an organisation chart.

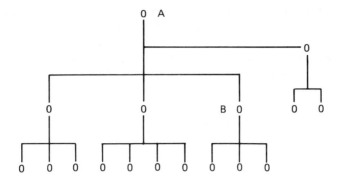

Figure 23   A formal organisation

Figure 24 superimposes some of the major *informal* channels on to the chart. We are producing what is sometimes called a *sociogram* which is a diagram which maps human interactions.

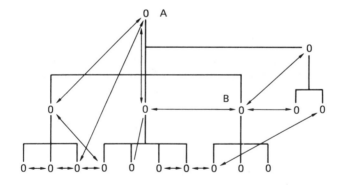

Figure 24   The informal structure superimposed on the formal structure

In this example, if we look carefully there seems to be two centres or loci of power rather than just one. Formally, B is A's subordinate but informally a good part of the organisation centres upon B with little reference to A.

To understand any organisation we have to understand both the formal and the informal. For anyone working within an organisation it is important to understand both. Often the two structures are so intertwined that it is impossible to separate and distinguish them.

Some organisations recognise the role of the informal to the extent that the formal structure is built around it. Ask why someone reports to so and so and you will receive the answer that 'it has always been the case', or that 'she gets on better with X rather than Y'. If we ask why many of our towns and cities are laid out as they are we find the answer is buried in history. The same is true for many of the relationships in organisations.

Why is there often a difference between formal and informal structures?

Formal structures are designed in order to:

- Carry out tasks.
- Be permanent.
- Fulfil the organisation's goals.

The structure has been consciously designed and has an official purpose.

Informal structures are not designed, they happen through human interactions. They exist to meet the human needs of the people who work in organisations. People are more than organisational units and have a wide variety of needs. Many of these needs such as those for friendship, affection and esteem can only be met through informal networks. We often find that people quite junior in the hierarchy have influence out of all proportion to their position because of their standing in the informal structure.

There is nothing intrinsically wrong with informal groups and informal structures. In fact, they can often be healthy and dynamic mechanisms for reinforcing organisational goals. If they fulfil needs in their members not met by the formal structure of work, then they have an important role in preventing frustration and resentment. But there are occasions when they can conflict with the official policy of the organisation. Informal groups or cabals may develop to impose their will on an organisation or to pursue a course of action in opposition to official policy.

The informal communication channels

Just as the formal organisation has its communications structure of meetings, memos, reports, notice boards and staff bulletins, the informal organisation has its own communications channels. Those of the informal organisation are generally oral and usually very fast in their operation.

The channels are known variously as the *grapevine, gossip* and *rumour*. Their important characteristic is that they cut across the divisions of the formal structure and usually are very powerful if the matters to be communicated are formally confidential or affect the future of particular individuals.

Some people believe that gossip should not be indulged in or listened to. However well-intentioned we might be, all of us do it. And often it is the only means of discovering what is happening. Some organisations seek to channel the grapevine for productive purposes by producing house magazines which allow issues to be raised publicly which would otherwise only become known through rumour.

CHAPTER 15

Organisational Concepts

In order to understand the way organisations operate, it is useful to understand a number of the key concepts underlying the structure. The following concepts are a vocabulary which will help you in being able to analyse and study the functioning of organisations.

ACCOUNTABILITY	AUTHORITY
BUREAUCRACY	HIERARCHY
DELEGATION	POWER
MANAGEMENT	SPAN OF CONTROL
MANAGEMENT STYLE	STATUS
RESPONSIBILITY	
STAFF & LINE	

Accountability

This is one of the major ideas holding the structure of organisations together. It can be thought of as a kind of organisational 'cement'. The idea is that every person has another person (or sometimes a group or committee) to whom he or she has to account for the proper discharge of responsibilities.

Accountability is present in every work role. Every person, whether at the most junior or the most senior level, has someone to whom he or she is accountable for doing the job properly.

In figure 25, A is directly accountable to his manager X for his work being carried out effectively. X is accountable to Y for the proper management of the work of X's section, which includes not only X's responsibilities but also those of A, B and C.

At the most senior level, the Managing Director, Chief Executive or whatever the title of the most senior person in the organisation is, will be accountable to a Board for the effective work of the whole organisation. In a company, accountability will be to a Board of Directors, if it is a local

116

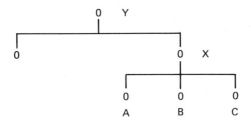

Figure 25

authority then the Chief Executive is accountable to the full Council and the Principal of your College is accountable to the Board of Governors (see figure 26).

Everybody has a boss, a person who has the responsibility to oversee his or her work; the Chairperson of the Board has the company's shareholders while the Prime Minister has to face the electorate for a renewal of the mandate at least every five years. The Governors of Colleges have an interesting accountability; they are accountable to the local authority which owns the College but they are also accountable to the community which the College serves.

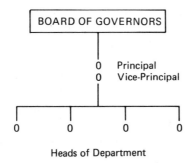

Figure 26   Accountability in a Further Education College

Activity: 'Accountability'

1. To whom are you accountable at College?
2. To whom are you accountable at work? (part-time students)
3. What organisations are represented on the Governing Body of your College?
4. To whom is the senior person in your company/organisation accountable to? (part-time students)

Authority

A question which is frequently asked of office holders is: "By what authority can you tell me to do such and such?" In order to carry out your responsibilities you require two things — *POWER* and *AUTHORITY*. In order to be able to exercise any degree of power in an organisation, an office-holder must have an official sanction for the exercise of that power.

Authority is the legitimate right to exercise power.

Sources of authority

The most important writer on authority in organisations was the German sociologist Max Weber (1864–1920). Weber was a student of social organisations and was interested in how organisations could direct the individuals in them towards given objectives. In order to direct people, those in senior positions require authority to legitimise the instructions and orders they give. It is because organisational members see their authority as legitimate that they are prepared to obey. According to Weber, the claims to legitimate authority are based on one or more of the following grounds:

1. *Traditional authority* — here claims to legitimacy are based on long-established beliefs and traditions. People obey others because 'they always have done so'. In many family-run businesses, the source of authority is of this kind.
2. *Charismatic authority* — this is where authority rests on the ability to motivate others by the strength of personality. Charisma is that aspect of personality which a few people possess which makes others follow them. Some modern businesses have bosses of this type. The traditional entrepreneur is often a person possessing charisma. The mass media and particularly television can create the aura of charisma around people of otherwise unexceptional personality. This is particularly the case in the worlds of politics, sport and entertainment.
3. *Rational and legal authority* — this is the source of authority in most organisations. Rational authority is that which is exercised by 'ex-

perts'. We buckle our seat belts on aeroplanes when the sign tells us to because we obey the commands of the expert — the pilot. Legal authority is that which rests on the rules of the organisation. The right of someone to exercise power is sanctioned by the organisation's rules.

Activity: 'Sources of authority'

What are the sources of authority which legitimise the actions of the following office holders? (The answers are given at the end of the chapter.)

A Police Officer	A Car Park Attendant	Your Boss
Your Course Tutor	The College Principal	You
The Archbishop of	The Prime Minister	A Judge
Canterbury	A Civil Servant	

Bureaucracy

In everyday usage, bureaucracy is synonymous with 'red tape' and inefficiency. However, there is a more technical meaning and one originated by Max Weber. For Weber, a bureaucracy was a special form of social organisation particularly associated with modern, large-scale industry and commerce.

What characterises bureaucracy is the rational and systematic way in which official duties are defined and distributed.

A bureaucracy exists where:

- There is a definition of responsibilities via job descriptions.
- Officials are given the power and authority to carry out tasks, but that power is limited by the rules which govern their office.
- The use of authority is not arbitrary but governed by rules.
- Competency of officials is ensured by proper selection and training so that they can effectively carry out their obligations and responsibilities.
- There is a carefully defined hierarchy of offices which can provide the organisation with continuity via recruitment from below. Work in the organisation provides individuals with a career and so is the main or sole source of income of its members.
- There is the proper maintenance of records and files.

We can see from this that in the technical sense most large and many small organisations can be described as bureaucracies. The civil service, banks, most large companies and local authorities display these characteristics. The major criticism of this approach to describing organisations is not that it is inaccurate but that it ignores all the informal and interpersonal aspects of organisations and concentrates too heavily on the formal aspects of work organisations.

Delegation

It is often said that delegation is the art of management. Simply, the need for delegation arises where one person feels it appropriate to ask a subordinate to carry out tasks which he or she would normally do. The need for delegation arises because

- A job-holder's role is overloaded.
- It is good staff development to ask a more junior member of staff to carry out tasks normally associated with more senior positions.

The problem with delegation for managers is how much to trust and how much to control the tasks which have been delegated. It is the case that even though tasks are delegated, the responsibility for those tasks cannot be. But you cannot expect another to carry out a task if he or she is constantly being observed by someone else.

Hierarchies

Most organisations are structured as hierarchies. That is to say, they are designed as tiers of managerial levels. In a hierarchy there is an unequal distribution of responsibility, power and authority with most of the power concentrated at the top of the pyramid.

> *A hierarchy exists when there is a system of people or things ranked into some kind of order. For organisations, this order is one of authority and accountability. If Mrs A is the Managing Director who has a subordinate Mr B who in turn manages a subordinate Miss C, then the set A–B–C is a hierarchy.*

The term 'hierarchy' suffers like that of 'bureaucracy' from having two meanings, a popular and a technical meaning. The popular use of hierarchical is of a system which is synonymous with the popular usage of bureaucratic. A hierarchy is seen as stultifying, rigid and caste-like. Many people believe that organisations should become non-hierarchical and be based on group and consensus decision-making. The technical term is one which concentrates on the fact that any form of ranking constitutes a hierarchy. In the technical sense it is perfectly possible for an organisation to have a hierarchical structure and to have popular and participatory decision-making. The hierarchical structure merely defines who is in charge of what and is accountable to whom.

Flat hierarchies and tall hierarchies

Some organisations are 'tall' in their structure while others are 'flat'. The distinction lies in the number of management layers an organisation has. Flat hierarchies have few layers of management with large spans of control (see figure 27). Tall hierarchies are characterised by small spans of control but with a large number of managerial levels (see figure 28).

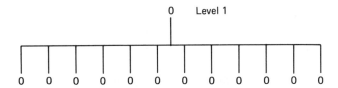

Figure 27   A flat hierarchy

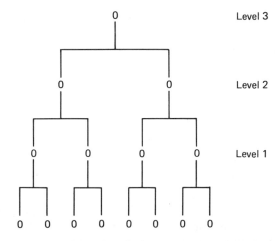

Figure 28   A tall hierarchy

Tall hierarchies are often seen as bureaucratic. Their multiple levels of management often involve rigidities which arise from the need to define roles and jobs rigorously in order that functions do not overlap. Communication between the top and the bottom of the organisation is often difficult. Senior managers may be remote from the majority of the staff. Delays in decision-making can be a difficulty as it takes time for problems at the bottom to come to the notice of people at the top, and for ideas at the top to percolate to the bottom.

However, despite these drawbacks there can be considerable bonuses. There is a great deal of scope for promotion and career development in a tall hierarchy. Because spans of control are smaller, then supervision can be more direct and the possibilities of genuine team work are available. The advantages of specialisation and the division of labour are available in tall hierarchies, and small and expert sections can easily be incorporated into them.

Flat hierarchies have fewer problems of communication between the top and the bottom. There are fewer status differentiations between organisation members and more opportunities for people at the bottom to influence those at the top. On the other hand, spans of control are larger in flat structures and unless organisational members are self-reliant there is the possibility that the level of supervision will be inadequate. Additionally, promotion and career development opportunities are lacking in these structures.

The best structure — flat or tall — depends upon the needs of the organisation. Each organisation operates differently, with different motives, priorities and goals. The structure should be tailored in such a way that it can most effectively pursue its aims. This view is known as the *CONTINGENCY APPROACH*. It states that there is no one correct way to manage or design an organisation, only a best way for each individual organisation. The right structure is *contingent*, that is to say depends, upon the wide range of factors including the competitive environment, the type of product, the quality of the labour force and the culture of the organisation.

Management

Management is the term given to the planning, controlling and decision-making functions within organisations. It is difficult to give any general definition of management as what constitutes management varies greatly between jobs and between organisations. A useful starting point is to divide management functions into personnel or people functions, task functions, and systems functions. Most managers will find themselves involved in some or all of the following.

Personnel/people functions

Selection and recruitment
Training and development
Counselling and advice
Disciplinary actions
Performance appraisal and assessment
Pay and bonus assessment

Task functions

Supervision and delegation
The definition of work roles and tasks
Product development
New business
Marketing and selling
Quality control

Systems functions

Communicating and informing
Budgeting and costing
Decision-making
Goal setting
Evaluation and review

Management style

The style in which management tasks can be carried out can vary enormously. Some managers take decisions after prolonged consultation with those involved while others have an authoritarian or dictatorial style.

Douglas McGregor in his book *The Human Side of the Enterprise* (1960) contrasts these two opposing styles as Theory X and Theory Y. The X managers are dictatorial in their approach and suspicious of their subordinates. They seek to control rather than to trust them. They believe that people have an inherent dislike of work and seek to avoid it when they can. As a result they impose tight and impersonal managerial controls over their subordinates. As they believe that human beings have little interest in their work other than their pay, they do not involve them in decision-making.

Theory Y managers by contrast take an optimistic view of human nature. They see people enjoying work if that work is fulfilling and satisfying. The manager's role is to improve the quality of the job so that people can make the best use of their talents and capabilities. They do not believe that people react to threats and bribes, but work best if they participate in decision-making. Theory Y managers see their job as releasing the talents of their subordinates by creating an environment where enterprise can flourish.

The only problem with this two-dimensional approach, which classifies management style as X or Y, authoritarian or participatory, is that it tends to assume that one style is right and the other is wrong. You should ask yourself whether there are not circumstances where a dictatorial approach may be more appropriate than a more open leadership style?

Another approach is to argue that the style of management which is the best for the situation is the one which produces the results. This is known as the *CONTINGENCY* approach to leadership style. Good leadership is seen as a relative or contingent process, which is to say that 'good leadership' is the type which works in a particular situation.

Contingent means 'dependent upon', and one writer on leadership, Fred Fiedler, has argued that the style of leadership a manager adopts should depend upon the situation he or she faces. The important variable for Feilder is the amount of power which the leader possesses, although the relationship between the leader and the team members and the nature of the task in hand are also important. Leaders need to adopt different styles depending upon the situation they face.

If a leader has little power but good personal relationships with the team, then it will make sense to manage through participation. On the other hand, if there is little sense of team spirit and poor performance but the leader has power, it would make sense to impose his or her views on the organisation.

Managers have to be certain that their style of leadership meets the situation they face. The important variables they need to keep in mind are:

- The demands of the task.
- The needs of the work groups.
- The needs of the individuals working in the organisation.

It is very probable that a style of management most appropriate to completing a particular task may not be the best suited to individual or group needs and vice versa. An intelligent manager will have to make a compromise between these different demands. It is the manager's job to decide on the priorities and to adopt the management style appropriate to reaching those goals. If the priority is team building, then a participatory style could work best, but if the priority is to cure poor or marginal performance then a more authoritarian approach may have to be adopted.

No manager should slavishly adopt a particular style. It is important when managing organisations to decide which are the areas which require tight controls and which are those where the controls can be loose. These areas may alter as personnel or situations change. The challenge of management is to be able to foresee the changes which are happening and to alter style accordingly.

Power

Power is a feature of all organisations. It is simply the ability which a person or group has to make others do what he, she or they want them to do. Power is often seen as a sinister concept. Of course, it can be and often is. But it is the way in which it is exercised which is the key. In many organisations, power relationships often go unnoticed because instructions and orders are often couched in polite terms — 'Could you, please, do this or that for me'. The power relationship underlies such an instruction because if an employee does not carry out the instruction then managers are entitled to exercise sanctions which are the manifestation of their power — the ultimate sanction being the sacking of an employee.

> *In organisations people are only given sufficient power to carry out their responsibilities effectively. In addition, organisational members require to be given the authority to exercise their powers.*

Charles Handy, in his book *Understanding Organisations*, has classified the forms of power available to members of organisations as follows.

Physical power

This is where force or the threat of it is used by someone to achieve his or her own ends. Organisation members never have the right to use physical sanctions (except in the case of the courts, prisons and other institutions of public safety). In industrial relations, physical force does on occasions manifest itself during strikes or lock outs when negotiations have broken down.

Resource power

Many managers possess this power. They may have the ability to decide how to allocate scarce resources, whether they are finances, promotions or new equipment.

Position power

This is sometimes called legal or legitimate power. As Handy puts it "the power that comes as a result of the role or position in the organisation." People who occupy certain roles have certain rights. It is such rights that allow managers to allocate work, control resources and provide the rights of access to various networks of information.

Expert power

This is power which arises from the possession of expert knowledge. As a source of power, it can only be claimed and used if others recognise and accept it as a source of power.

Personal power

This is often called charisma and it is the power of personality. It is like expert power in that it can only be exercised if others recognise and accept it.

Negative power

This is the power to stop things happening or to delay or disrupt them. Many people in organisations have the power to delay or distort developments. Trade Unions often use this source of power when negotiations break down during collective bargaining.

Responsibility

Work is all about responsibility: the duties and commitments which we are required to undertake during our working day. Responsibility goes hand in hand with accountability because all role holders are accountable to their superior for the exercise of those responsibilities. In addition, it is not something that can be delegated and employees cannot escape their responsibility by delegation.

Span of control

Span of control refers to the number of persons for whom a manager has direct responsibility. In figure 29, A has a span of control of four, and B and C spans of control of three people each.

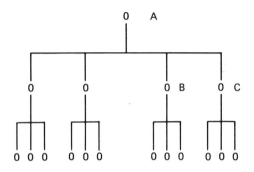

Figure 29

There is much debate about the optimum span of control. Much depends upon the type of work and the sort of people employed. Unskilled trainees will require a great deal of supervision and so efficient management will call for a smaller span of control than a situation where the employees are experienced. Usually, self-motivated professionals require little supervision and so in such circumstances spans of control can be large.

Staff and line

Line management roles refer to those positions which are directly concerned with the operational aspects of the business (see figure 30). Functions such as production, sales, accounting and purchasing are all concerned with the making and selling of a product.

Staff functions on the other hand are those which provide common services to an organisation (see figure 30). The canteen, the personnel department, maintenance and central computing services usually fall into that category. They are provided centrally in order to make the most effective use of resources and to give line managers the freedom to do the jobs they are paid to do.

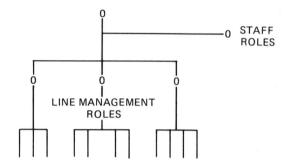

Figure 30

Activity: 'College organisation chart'

Draw an organisation chart of your College. You should clearly distinguish between line and staff functions. In order to do this you need to consider whether a particular department, section or function is *directly* concerned with the main operational function of the College. The operational function is the provision of teaching and learning opportunities for students.

Status

Status is an important concept in any consideration of how organisations work. Generally, it is the case that the positions at the apex of the hierarchy have more power, authority and status than those lower down. Status is defined in terms of values and norms. People and their roles have status because other people assign it to them.

Status is usually enhanced with a range of symbols which express status to others. The size of offices, the type and size of office furniture such as desks, reserved car parking spaces, titles and badges of rank are just some of the ways in which status is expressed.

Are status and status symbols really necessary? To answer this question you need to distinguish between status that is earned and that which is not. If people are accorded status because of the respect in which their achievements are held, then status may be regarded as a normal part of social life. But, of course, some status symbols merely seek to inflate the importance of an office or a person out of all proportion to his or her achievements or responsibilities.

Status can be an important motivator. Many people struggle for promotion in order to enhance their status within organisations.

Answers to 'Sources of authority' activity on page 119

A Police Officer	Legal/Rational and Traditional Authority
A Car Park Attendant	Legal Authority
Your Boss	This will depend on your business but it is likely to be Legal/Rational
Your Course Tutor	Rational Authority
The College Principal	Rational/Legal Authority
You	It depends upon your role, but if you are at work is likely to be Legal/Rational
The Archbishop of Canterbury	Traditional Authority
The Prime Minister	Legal/Rational, Traditional, Charismatic
A Judge	Legal/Rational, Traditional
A Civil Servant	Legal/Rational

CHAPTER 16

Meetings

'Meetings, Bloody Meetings' is the title of a well-known training film produced by Video Arts Ltd, and it may well be shown to you on your course. Its title sums up the attitude of many people to what is an essential feature of working life — namely, meetings. Managers may spend as much as fifty per cent of their working lives engaged in meetings of various types. It is usually the case that the more senior people are, the more meetings they have to attend. We need to ask why meetings are so essential. The rationale for working with others in meetings of all types is based on the following:

- They enable people to pool ideas.
- They are means of settling disputes.
- They can bring conflict into the open.
- They enable consensus to be reached.
- They co-ordinate activities.
- They are a means of informing others.
- They offer opportunities for participation in decision-making.
- They are a useful vehicle to test out ideas before implementation.
- They are a vehicle for accountability.
- They are a means of formulating policies.

If meetings are potentially so useful, then why do so many go wrong? In order to answer this we need to understand what makes so many meetings ineffectual and time-wasting, and to formulate means by which the meetings you attend can be as productive as possible. During your course you will be involved in a wide range of activities which will involve you in meetings both formal and informal. You need to develop the skills to run and to participate in successful meetings. A very good way is to start by keeping notes of your observations about the running and the outcomes of meetings you attend.

Some of the points to look out for are:

'Was the meeting well chaired?'
'Did the meeting have a clear purpose?'
'Did the participants know why they were participating?'
'Did the meeting have an agenda?'
'Was the agenda kept to?'
'Were clear decisions reached?'
'Were the decisions recorded?'
'Did the meeting drag on longer than it needed to?'
'Was the bulk of the time devoted to the important or the trivial agenda items?'
'Did some people dominate the meeting, and if so, why?'
'What roles did particular participants play?'
'What role did you play in the meeting?'
'Were all the participants playing an active and positive role?'

Types of meetings

The main types of meetings are:

Problem-solving meetings. This type of meeting concentrates on tackling problems and making decisions. There are usually shared objectives in the meeting — at least that the problem should be solved.

Negotiation meetings. At this type of meeting there are usually two sides who are trying to make an agreement or bargain over a point. In such a meeting the two sides usually have different objectives.

Selling meetings. In this type of meeting one person or party is trying to persuade the others to a particular point of view. The objective of the persons doing the convincing is to 'sell' their ideas to others.

Command meetings. This meeting is called by a manager to inform his subordinates or to instruct or to control them. The manager specifies the objectives.

Communications/advisory meetings. This is an exchange of views and opinions. Its major objective is to seek opinions so that a manager can take a decision at a later stage.

Support meetings. Many meetings help individuals and groups to overcome their particular problems or fulfil an emotional need. The objectives will be personal to the individual members.

One problem with meetings is that they are not all of one type. It is important to know what type of meeting is best for a particular purpose and to make certain that the participants know the purpose and status of the meeting. People often become frustrated if they are uncertain about why a meeting has been called, what it is for and why they are there. Expectations have to be met if people are to be satisfied with their experience of a meeting. If people expected to come to a meeting to make a decision, they will feel let down if the meeting does not reach one. Meetings do not have to be decision-making. A meeting which just airs views is quite legitimate but every one present should be aware of it.

Committee meetings

Most organisations of any size work through a system of committees. They have the function of making policies, taking decisions, and co-ordinating activities. They are an essential element in the management process and they provide the means of participation of various interests.

Committees are formal and follow rules of procedure. The main features of committees are:

- They elect or have appointed a person who *chairs* the meeting. The Chair conducts the meeting, interprets the rules and makes certain that the business of the meeting is effectively and properly conducted. (Until recently the title Chairman was given to the person chairing meetings. This title is still the one in general use but the moves towards non-discriminatory, non-sexist language have led to the use of titles such as *Chairperson*, and the more neutral *Chair*. The title Chair is useful in that it separates the formal role from the person occupying it.)
- They has a *Secretary*, whose role is to record the proceedings and the decisions of the meetings and to publish the minutes of the meetings and the agenda with any supporting papers.
- They have a *written agenda*, which is generally published in advance together with the *Notice of the Meeting* (see figure 31). This provides the timetable for the meeting and allows members of the committee to prepare themselves in advance for the discussions that will take place. (The control of the agenda can be one of the most important powers which the Chair exercises by deciding the order of the discussion and whether or not a particular issue is a legitimate topic of debate.)

A typical committee meeting has the following structure:

(a) Apologies for absence from members unable to attend.
(b) The signing of the minutes of the previous meeting prepared by the Secretary as a correct record of the proceedings.
(c) Matters arising from the minutes. This allows the meeting to ask questions, comment or review what happened at previous meetings

and to check that decisions have been carried out, or that matters have progressed in the manner envisaged.

(d) The business items of the meeting. These items form the bulk of the business of the committee.

(e) Any other business allows matters to be raised which are not on the agenda. Some committees refuse to allow non-agenda items, while others only allow matters notified to the Chair before the meeting. The value of AOB is to allow urgent matters to be raised which cannot wait until the next meeting.

Notice of Meeting

To: The Members of the Policy Committee
From: G K Browne (Secretary)

The next meeting of the Policy Committee will be held on Friday 25th May at 1030, in the Board Room.

Agenda

1. Apologies for Absence.
2. Welcome to new members.
3. Minutes of the Meeting of the 7th April (copy attached).
4. Matters arising from the Minutes.
5. Exchange of information.
6. Proposal for Building Works.
7. Production Quotas for new models for the next financial year — a preliminary discussion. (Papers will be available at the the the meeting.)
8. Paper from K Stuart on the Reorganisation of the Committee Structure (copy attached).
9. Date of next meeting.
10. Any other business.

Figure 31   A typical Notice of Meeting and Agenda

Some meetings have an exchange of information session after the discussion of the minutes. This allows members to give a brief review of events on topics of interest to other members, and to update the progress of these events since the previous meeting.

Some committees may have a correspondence item in which they consider and suggest replies to important items of correspondence recieved. This item often appears on the agendas of the committees of clubs, societies and voluntary organisations.

Formal committees have *rules of procedure* which govern the way in which the meeting operates. The rules may be laid down in Standing Orders or may be the custom and practice of the organisation. The Chair interprets and enforces the rules of the meeting. It is the duty of the Chair to make certain the procedures are adhered to. The rules usually applied to meetings are:

- That the Agenda order is strictly adhered to unless a motion is made to alter the order.
- That members of the Committee speak through the Chair. This means that all remarks have to be addressed to the Chair. It means that only one person can speak at a time and that members cannot address each other directly. This prevents personal discussions and arguments developing freely and allows the Chair to retain control of the meeting.
- Decisions are usually reached upon a motion being put to the meeting.
- If a visible consensus is not reached, then decisions are taken on a majority vote. The Chair has the casting vote in the case of a tie.

Accountability in committee meetings lies with the whole membership and not with particular individuals. Final agreement is the agreement of all, not just the members who are in favour of a particular motion.

The 'hidden agenda'

We have described how meetings can have a variety of objectives and be used for a number of tasks, and we have described the procedures which normally govern the operation of formal meetings. What we have not done is to describe 'what really goes on'. You may ask 'but surely the minutes will tell us what went on?', and up to a point they do — in the formal sense.

There are two structures operating in any meeting and these may be classified as follows.

(1) The *'surface structure'*. This is what the meeting is notionally about, or as we have already described it, the formal structure. A meeting to decide next year's budget is formally about just that — fixing the budget. The minutes will be entirely concerned with just these items, but in almost all meetings something else is happening.

(2) The *'deep structure'*. The 'something else' that happens in meetings is sometimes called the informal structure and it is about the politics of decision-making. The interplay of personalities plays a considerable part here. If we take our budget-fixing example and examine it for a moment, we realise that two separate things may be going on. On the

surface there is the process of deciding which department in the organisation will have what to spend next year. Complex formulas will often be employed to show how impersonal and objective the decision-making has been. Underlying this scientific calm will often be the interplay of personalities and politics. Departmental managers, wanting a larger share of the cake, may feel aggrieved about the effect of the formulas on their plans, and may be jealous of those who appear to be doing well out of the process. A manager may support another manager's position and justify it according to organisational criteria, but underneath the solidarity may lie the expectation of being supported later in the meeting.

The 'hidden agenda' is the name often given to this covert process whereby liaisons and alliances are formed for mutual support, and battle lines are drawn. It is often complained of by many that a meeting will take five minutes to agree the expenditure of ten million and two hours to debate a minor item worth only a few thousand. The hidden agenda helps to explain although not to justify it. Often the trivial item is one on which a person's reputation, promotion or future prospects depend.

To be successful at meetings you need to know what is *really* going on, or in other words what is below the surface. What are the forces, who may combine with you or against you and why? You need to know the trade-offs from support, the costs of failure, and the price to be paid in attacking a view. An all-out attack by a junior on a senior at a meeting is usually costly, especially if the junior member wins. That junior may have to pay for the victory with a heavy defeat in the future. Senior managers cannot afford to lose face too often and will bide their time to re-assert their authority.

You may ask whether there has to be these two levels at meetings. The answer is that there does not but, in practice, there is usually a strong element of politics. A few very mature groups can meet together and are able to state openly how they feel without their feelings being manipulated or exploited by other members. In such meetings the deep structures rise to the surface and form part of the main agenda. Committees who wish to operate in this fashion have to avoid their members playing games or having manipulative strategies. They have to work to fulfil, as far as possible, the genuine needs of their members. In such situations, assertive team members who are able to state a strong case but appreciate the genuine needs of others are necessary. The other difference is the absence of the competitive winning and losing. The outcome of mature meetings is to search for solutions and to reach consensus, not for a particular group to score points over another.

Taking minutes

The minutes of a meeting are the record of the proceedings and the proposed actions which have been decided. They are taken by the Secretary, although the actual recording activity may be delegated to a Minute Secretary or Committee Clerk. If you are given this task it is best to write the minutes up the same day or as soon as possible after the meeting while the discussion is still fresh in your mind.

There is a special responsibility which the Secretary has and that is to make certain that the minutes are accurate. Once the next meeting has approved them, they form the official record of what happened and what was decided. There is no going back and so they must be accurate and precise.

Minutes must contain all the facts about a meeting. When and where it met, the times it opened and closed, the people who were present, apologies for absence, actions it was agreed should be taken and the names of the individuals who will take responsibility. Some minutes are very full and contain verbatim quotes while others only record the decisions and the actions required. The later 'decisions only' approach helps to prevent members from making long speeches which they can read in the minutes. It is important to number all of the items in the minutes so that it is easy to refer to particular items at a later date.

How to be successful at meetings

Be organised. Successful committee members are properly and thoroughly prepared for the meetings they attend. Read all the papers you are sent, before attending the meeting. Mark passages to which you want to refer or where you wish to seek clarification.

Be punctual for meetings. Nothing creates a worse impression than people who are late for meetings.

Take notes during meetings. You should not rely on your memory about important issues or decisions. Minutes of meetings do not always record all of the details which were discussed. Your notes should be brief and to the point. Taking notes helps concentration, particularly during long meetings.

Pay particular attention to the wording of minutes. It is very easy for a Secretary to fail to capture the feeling of a meeting when he or she writes up the minutes. Compare the minutes with your own notes and raise any discrepancies.

Find support for your ideas. You may need to form alliances for your ideas. It is sometimes worth lobbying other members beforehand if you want support on an issue. Remember that other people will expect your support in return for backing you.

Keep to the point. Nothing is more irritating than people who do not keep to the point and talk for too long. You are more likely to influence others if you make your points clearly, forcefully and succinctly.

Be watchful of the tactics of others. There are a variety of ways of defeating a proposal other than directly speaking against it. You may find your opponents talking at length of earlier items on the agenda or have late items postponed to a later meeting, or talking off the issue in order to divert the discussion. You are likely to make a success of meetings by recognising when others are using tactics such as these. You may need to remind the Chair of the length of the agenda or the point at issue if a speaker is not keeping to the matter at issue.

CHAPTER 17

Information Systems

The term 'information system' refers to ways in which the information available to an organisation is used, stored, retrieved and accessed. Any organisation needs to utilise as much of the information at its disposal as it can, and to use that information effectively to aid decision-making. In the seventeenth century the philosopher Francis Bacon coined the saying 'Knowledge is Power'. In the late twentieth century this could be rephrased as 'Information is Power'.

> The term 'system' refers to the interdependence of the parts which make up a whole. The components are affected by being part of the system and change as other elements of it change. Computer systems refer to the hardware, software and the manual aspects of data handling and storage.

All businesses process huge quantities of information every day of the week. Invoices, bills, memos, production figures, personnel reports, absentee returns and customer complaints pass in, out and around the organisation and are stored and filed away. Potentially, there are vast opportunities for using this data to make decisions and to look for trends and significant relationships between seemingly unconnected happenings. In some businesses, however, instead of this information providing opportunities the sheer bulk of the data is a burden and a *liability*. It becomes a mass of paperwork which chokes the workings of the organisation. Its use becomes limited to the function with which it is directly connected and it is not tied into a system of management information.

The data received and generated by an organisation can be an *asset*. It needs to be properly organised and, nowadays, this usually requires a computerised system to handle it. A properly designed information system allows information to be catalogued so that it is easy to access and use.

In order that an information system can operate efficiently and effectively, an organisation has to take the following factors into account:

- It must consider the most effective ways of *handling* data.
- It must decide on the best ways of *storing* data.
- It must decide on the best method of *processing* data.
- It must make decisions on its *information requirements*.
- It must ensure that those who need the data can *access* it.

Until comparatively recently, the amount of investment in office techno-logy was relatively small compared with other areas of business. This is changing and businesses now realise the vast potential for effective decision-making which the efficient use of information provides.

Levels of information

Information is not all of one type, and different levels and functions within the organisation have varying requirements (see figure 32).

Senior management requires information in order to base policy-decisions and to plan. It needs information in order to provide it with a degree of certainty about the results of decision-making.

At the middle management level, information is required about the efficiency of the operation. There is a need to know whether sales are on target, and whether the quality of products is up to specification. Informa-tion is required to ensure that the operation is effectively organised.

At the clerical level, it is important that records and files are accurately maintained. A customer may have a query about an order and the original needs to be looked up in the records.

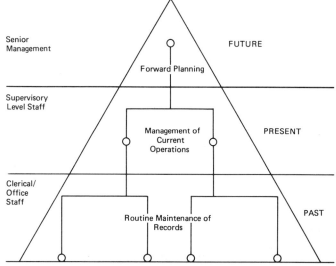

Figure 32 Information requirements in an organisation

Too much information

One of the features of modern business life is 'information overload'. Rather than moving towards the 'paperless office', which analysts were forecasting in the 1970s, many people in business are in danger of being swamped by the amount of paper created by the volume of information available to them. Mailshot advertising, computer printouts, sales data, budget forecasts, performance monitoring data, business journals and specialist magazines are just some of the sources of information which have to be read and absorbed. The difficulty in many offices is how to deal with the work that increased information brings.

In order to be efficient, you have to find ways of deciding which information is important and which can go straight in the waste paper basket. Not all of it can be read at once. There is a need to decide what information to store and the most effective means of retrieving it. The solution of ignoring most of it is not an ideal option.

In order to decide what information is of value, you have to decide what it is you want to know and for what purpose. A constant theme in this book is that you must plan and decide upon your priorities. This is particularly true when it comes to information handling. Some advertising circulars, brochures and catalogues are invaluable to you while others are worthless. Only you know what you want to achieve. The month by month sales figures may make fascinating reading but, if they do not apply to your job, should you waste your time reading them? You should file them, as they may be an important reference at a later date. If you do not order furniture, then do not even bother to open the office equipment magazines.

The next stage, once you have sorted out what is important, is to decide how best to store and retrieve it. The terms 'storage' and 'retrieval' sound rather grand, but the fact is that despite computers those terms still, in reality, mean *filing*. This may not sound like an important topic but it is one of the keys to being well organised. If you can always lay your hands on the necessary information, you will always appear to be in command of situations.

Why file?

We file information and documents to

- Preserve documents and keep them clean and tidy.
- Have essential information available for easy reference.

A good filing system is essential for any office and this means that documentation should be stored and catalogued in an efficient manner. Before we discuss the various different systems of filing, we need to make some points about dealing with documentation in business. The essential points to note are:

- It is necessary to keep documents up to date. Important documents should always be on top of the pile. It is too easy for important matters to languish at the bottom of an in-tray or in a drawer. You need a 'bring forward system' which constantly brings important matters to the fore for action.
- If documents are borrowed from files or from the office, make certain a note is kept concerning where and to whom they went. It is often necessary to obtain a signature for borrowed documents.
- 'Diarise' important matters. This awful sounding term is a useful method of bringing important matters forward by entering them in a diary so that you know when your deadlines are. A wall-mounted year planner is another useful method of planning for deadlines.

Filing systems

The main conventions for classifying files or documents for storage are as follows:

Alphabetical
Alpha-numerical
Chronological
Geographical
Numerical
Subject

Alphabetical

With this system, documents are arranged in *alphabetical order*. For example, the files are arranged according to the first letter of a surname and each subsequent letter as in the example below.

Saint F. O.
Salis A.
Sallis K.
Salmon B. E.
Salter A. C.

If several surnames are the same, then the system is file by initials.

  Jones A. B.
  Jones F. A.
  Jones F. T.
  Jones V. B.

A problem often arises when a document needs to be filed in more than one place. A letter for Salmon, for instance, may contain an important reference to Jones. The solution is to put a sheet of paper in one file marked 'Jones cross reference Salmon' in the Jones file or 'see under . . . '. Another method is to photocopy the document and to file it twice, but to make certain that it is marked with its cross reference.

Alpha-numerical

This is a system which combines letters and numbers. For example XJ — 7364, AS — 738.

Chronological

Chronological classification involves filing by date order. It is usual to file all the correspondence under a particular heading by this method. It is a sensible practice to place the latest information on the front of the file. This is a useful method for filing miscellaneous correspondence and memoranda.

Geographical

This simply means having all the files in alphabetical order under a geographical location. For instance, a company may have its sales area divided into East, Central, West and North and correspondence may be filed under these headings.

Numerical

This system is often used when numbers are given to particular jobs. A garage, for example, may file information about customers under the registration number of their customers' vehicles.

Subject

In this system, documents are classified according to their subject. Subjects are filed alphabetically.

The same classification systems apply when data is being stored on a computerised database. The advantage of computerised storage methods is that more elaborate cross referencing is possible, and data pertinent to a number of files can be updated by a single key stroke.

Information sources

In addition to the information available from an organisation's own files, it is possible nowadays to obtain information from a wide variety of sources. Businesses have always been able to call upon the resources of specialist libraries, many of them run by professional or trade bodies such as the British Institute of Management, the Chartered Institute of Public Finance and Accountancy and government departments and agencies. Organisations also receive information and intelligence from their membership of trade associations, professional bodies and local business groups such as Chambers of Commerce. For a fee, a number of private research organisations provide strategic information on markets, the economy, and customer and financial trends. Good examples include the Economist Intelligence Unit, The Henley Centre for Forecasting, and Financial Times Business Information. Advice on exporting can be obtained from British Embassies and High Commissions abroad, the British Overseas Trade Board and the Institute of Export, among other specialist bodies.

Trade directories

Most types of business have a trade association to provide services to their members. One such service is trade directories. They provide data on other members, suppliers, customers and other useful information. Such directories are sometimes available to non-members for a fee and can be found in specialist libraries. A good example is the *Times 1000* which provides an annual update on the leading companies in the UK and abroad.

Research information

There are a considerable number of consultants providing a vast range of information and data. Market research is undertaken by organisations such as Gallup, NOP, Marplan and MORI. The BBC through BBC Data Enquiry Service sells the information it holds on social, political and economic aspects of countries worldwide. Such a service can be useful to a company which is considering exporting and so is interested in general market information.

A wide range of organisations offer various forms of business consultancy, including employment selection, training needs analysis, market intelligence, organisational design and motivational research.

On-line services

Today, much of the information available in libraries and directories is available on-line. Databases are available to subscribers who need only a telephone, a modem and a microcomputer to be able to key into a wide range of information services. An interesting example for large organisations is Euronet–Diane, started in 1979 by the telecommunication authorities of the European Community. Diane stands for Direct Information Access Network in Europe. It contains several databases covering trade and commercial information. Subscribers are limited to large organisations but there are other similar database services for smaller companies.

Videotex services

Many of you will be familiar with British Telecom's Prestel, BBC's Ceefax and the IBA's Oracle service. They are known variously as Viewdata, Videotex and Teletext services. In addition there are a number of private subscriber services.

The largest system in the world is Prestel whose customers include small firms, colleges, schools, banks, retail stores and private individuals.

The information on Prestel, and there is currently over 300,000 pages of it from 1000 organisations, is displayed on a monitor which can be a television set. The subscriber also needs a microcomputer, a telephone line and a modem (to connect the computer to the telephone system) and the necessary software.

The subscriber can access information from government departments, educational organisations, major companies and other bodies such as the Stock Exchange, the London International Future Exchange, and the Consumer Associations. You can find out Travel Information such as the times of flights or the departure of inter-city trains.

Those of you studying Travel and Tourism units will be familiar with the Prestel information accessible to travel agents who can access information on the availability of holidays, seats on aeroplanes and package holidays.

Organisations can obtain a printout of Prestel pages displayed on their monitors.

Ceefax and Oracle provide less in the way of business information than Prestel, but do provide useful news and travel services. They provide stock market, commodity prices and exchange rate movement information.

The advantages of subscription information to an organisation, whether it is provided in the form of directories or via computerised systems, is that of cost and availability. In terms of cost-effectiveness, companies need only pay for the services they require and are saved the enormous cost of research and cataloguing information. They can also tap into information which no firm, however large, could afford to provide for itself.

The impact of Information Technology

For many large companies today, information technology (IT) has become the basis of their business. Tour operators, credit and charge card companies, banks and finance companies, to name only a few business sectors, could not operate on their present mass scale without the power which Information Technology and Computing provides for them. Over 80 per cent of package holidays are booked via on-line viewdata systems in travel agencies, which enables tour operators to book thousands of holidays an hour at key times during the year.

The 'Big Bang' which revolutionised trading in financial markets in the City of London in 1986 could not have happened without the use of sophisticated computerised trading systems. More and more organisations are discovering the importance of IT to their business. Supermarket chains have discovered the necessity of major computer installations to control checkouts and to monitor and replenish stock.

For this reason, many managements now build IT into their strategic planning. That is to say that when they decide on their forward planning, over say the next five to ten years, they do so with a view to the impact which technological developments will make on their products and markets. Companies are realising that information technology and services should be linked to the marketing function when planning their long-term strategy.

Of equal importance to recognising the importance of IT to the future prospects of a company is recognising the need to train people in IT developments. People will be motivated to use IT if they have the competencies to operate it. Successful companies are those which spend money on training their workforces to be flexible and to be excited by new technological innovations.

Many employees are concerned and worried by the rapid pace of technological change. They fear the outdating of their skills and redundancy. Such feelings lead to low morale and poor motivation. In order to utilise the potential of IT, organisations require the opposite — high motivation and enthusiasm — among their employees. Many companies have a structured programme of training which provides all the workforce with a cycle of updating relevant to their needs. This is usually coupled with the opportunity to learn and to use newly acquired skills.

Training is the principal means of compensating for skill losses and in helping redeployment. It helps to cut redundancy to a minimum and it maintains the morale and the motivation of the workforce.

CHAPTER 18

Management Services

Methods of change

Change within organisations can be either *reactive* or *proactive*. The former approach is illustrated by the company who suddenly cancels the Christmas party and the annual staff bonus because of a downturn in the market when only three months earlier it was recruiting new staff. Reactive change occurs when organisations are forced to react to external or internal pressures. Crisis management is another name given to it.

Proactive change, by contrast, is planned change. With proactive change, alterations only take place as part of a carefully orchestrated policy designed to meet a number of clear and well thought out objectives. Clearly, this approach is superior to the making of reactive adjustments. This section seeks to explore the methods an organisation can use to ensure that its structures and procedures are up to date and fulfilling the criteria required for successful change.

Managing by objectives

Management by Objectives, or MbO for short, is the process by which an organisation can establish clear objectives. These objectives might include:

- To maximise profits.
- To increase market share by 20% over the next year.
- To improve the quality of its products.
- To increase employee participation in the decision-making process.

Once objectives have been established for the whole organisation, they are broken down into a series of goals and strategies. After this, plans are drafted to provide the means of reaching the goals. An example of how objectives are transformed into plans of action is shown in the following example:

Objective	— To increase market share by 20%
Goals	— To increase the sales of product A by 5000 by September 19. . To expand the sales of product B by 8000 in South-east Region.
Strategic Plan	— An advertising campaign for product A based on advertising in the trade press and concentrating on a range of discounts available on the product in spring.
	The expansion of Product B is to be achieved by a telephone sales campaign in the South-east Region. The upgraded nature of the product will be the major feature of the campaign. The emphasis will be on increasing sales to existing customers.

In a system of management by objectives, each of these sets of objectives, goals and plans will be mirrored by a set of objectives and plans established at each organisation level. In this way each department, section and individual employee will specify or have specified how they are to achieve their particular part of the overall *CORPORATE PLAN*.

Each employee will have his or her own personal targets and these will usually be the result of an annual appraisal interview which will help individuals to see how they fit into the total picture. To be successful, individuals, departments and the organisation will require performance measures which will help the monitoring process, which in turn helps to ensure that the organisation is on target.

MbO can only operate effectively if it is systematically organised, and if the communication system can accurately translate the corporate objectives into individual objectives. Decision-making processes need to be clear and efficient, and it is important that there is a high level of motivation among the people working in the organisation. People must be able to identify with the corporate objectives and want to carry them out. The organisation, for its part, must reward individual efforts which result in the goals being achieved.

One important aspect of this type of approach is to have an efficient and effective organisation with procedures and practices which allow for the achievement of objectives. In order to achieve a 'well-oiled' system, an organisation needs to have its functions systematically reviewed and monitored, and to undergo periodic 'health checks'. This is the role of Organisation and Method studies.

Organisation and Methods

Organisation and Methods, or O & M for short, is the name given to the independent appraisal of the efficiency and effectiveness of the operations of an organisation. It may be carried out by a Management Services Unit or Division, if it is a large outfit, although many firms employ external consultants to do the work for them.

Organisation and Methods

"A management service, the object of which is to increase the administrative efficiency of an organisation by improving procedures, methods and systems, communications and controls and organisation structures"

British Standards Institution
No. 3138

In recent years a new variant of O & M has appeared known as *Systems Analysis*. The work is often related to the investigation of computer systems but work on manual systems is often undertaken, although usually with the brief of considering whether computerisation will improve efficiency. A systems analyst is a person whose role is to undertake a continual appraisal of the working of procedures and systems within an organisation. In this chapter we will investigate systems analysis within the context of O & M.

The aims of Organisation and Methods

- To increase the overall *effectiveness* of the organisation to meet its objectives.
- To increase the *efficiency* of the organisation by reducing the cost of its operation.
- To *investigate* and *document* the existing procedures within the organisation.

The important points to note about O & M is that it is a logical and systematic study designed to place the workings of an organisation under close scrutiny. The idea of fully documenting a system is to see whether it is the best way of doing things or whether an alternative method would be more effective or efficient.

How O & M is carried out

Those of you who are at work and are employed by large organisations
such as banks, insurance companies or local authorities may well have had
first hand experience of O & M. Your job will probably have been graded
as the result of *job evaluation*; your department or section will have been
mapped on an *organisation chart*; *the forms* you work with will have been
carefully produced to provide the necessary information for a variety of
users; and the *way you work* may also have been the subject of analysis.
While reading this paragraph you may have come to the conclusion that
this book could have been retitled as a guide to systems analysis and
O & M for what we are doing in it is to examine how organisations work
and the way that work affects the people who are employed in them.

Organisation and Methods is a skilled occupation and analysts need
considerable expertise and tact. Many people resent outsiders 'telling them
how to do their jobs', and it is all too easy to make people feel insecure so
that they put up barriers to change if they consider that their jobs are being
threatened. Nevertheless, an organisation cannot avoid the process of
analysis. Managers must commission research into the effectiveness of
operations. As an organisation develops so must the systems which it
operates, but there is a danger that it can become strangled with 'spaghetti-
like' procedures which grow in an unplanned manner and threaten to
choke the very work they are supposed to facilitate.

Organisation and Methods analysts need the trust and support of those
working in the organisation if they are to produce effective solutions to
problems. In return they need to explain what they are doing, why they are
doing it, and the benefits which analysis and change can bring to both the
organisation and the individuals within it.

The following types of investigation are frequently carried out by
O & M analysts:

Organisational design. This work may involve the analysis of the accountability structure, the division of responsibilities, the chain of command, the
length of spans of control and the manner in which duties are distributed.
The starting point for this work is usually the drawing up of an organisation
chart and the preparation or updating of job descriptions. The usual way in
which this work is carried out is by *interview* and *observation*. Usually the
analyst has prepared interview forms and questionnaires to make certain
that all the points relating to formal relationship are properly covered in
any discussions. This is what is meant by a logical and systematic approach
to organisational analysis.

Clerical system surveys. Clerical work systems are extremely important to
the effective functioning of any organisation. When we discuss organisations, it is all too easy to concentrate on major policy decisions at Board

level and forget about the routine systems. The effective operation of routine systems is crucial to customers, clients and suppliers. Organisational success depends on how well it can process orders, chase enquiries and invoice clients. Most of this work is a matter of clerical routine. To ensure that clerical work procedures operate effectively, O & M analysts use *flowcharts* and *document analysis charts*. Figure 33 shows some symbols used in flowcharting work, and figure 34 the breakdown of the procedure for interviewing a student, after application for a place at a College.

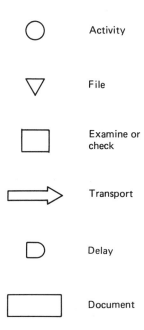

These standard systems are used to flowchart the operation of systems. The reason is to provide a logical and pictorial representation of the system. From this it is easy to trace how the system works, and whether there are unnecessary steps or wasteful duplication.

Figure 33   O & M symbols

The clerical work analysis involves breaking a job down into its component elements. This may involve elements of *work study* or *work measurement* whereby a particular operation is timed, and that time

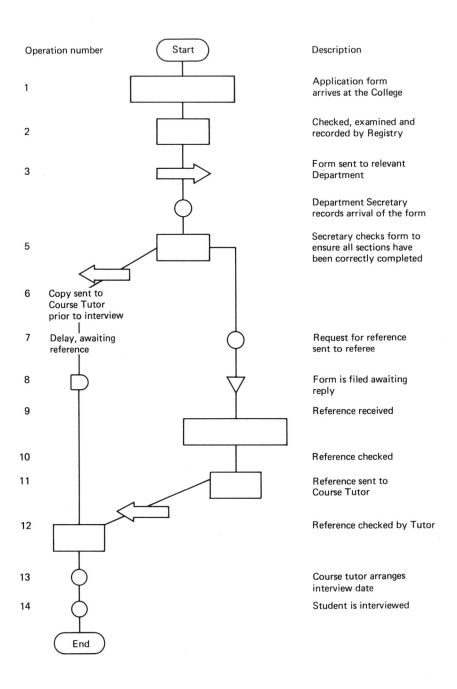

Operation number | Start | Description

1 — Application form arrives at the College

2 — Checked, examined and recorded by Registry

3 — Form sent to relevant Department

— Department Secretary records arrival of the form

5 — Secretary checks form to ensure all sections have been correctly completed

6 Copy sent to Course Tutor prior to interview

7 Delay, awaiting reference — Request for reference sent to referee

8 — Form is filed awaiting reply

9 — Reference received

10 — Reference checked

11 — Reference sent to Course Tutor

12 — Reference checked by Tutor

13 — Course tutor arranges interview date

14 — Student is interviewed

End

Figure 34 Student application procedure

compared with previously produced standard tables. This provides a means of discovering by how much the actual operation differs from the norm. Work measurement may mean researching the amount of physical movement which any particular individual does in carrying out a task. A person may have to rise from a chair; walk ten feet to a counter to answer a query from a client; walk to a filing cabinet to find information; walk to a table to pick up the necessary forms; and then return to the counter. The O & M analyst might suggest that the filing cabinet be moved next to the counter and the forms placed on a shelf beneath it. The objective would be to eliminate unnecessary and wasteful movement.

O & M analysts are concerned with *form design* and their interest is to ensure that business forms are correctly designed so that information is conveyed in an orderly manner, and that end users can easily find the information they require. The analyst will consider whether forms need to be printed on NCR paper which provides multi-copies, and if so how many are required. It is important to consider what the form is for, who will be using it, and what it is being used to record.

Job Evaluation

So far in this book we have discussed hierarchies in organisations and the roles which people occupy in them. What has not been discussed up to now is why particular jobs are located where they are in a hierarchy and why one job may be ranked as more senior to another and meriting a higher rate of pay. In some companies the establishment of the hierarchy of work roles is the result of custom and practice, but in other organisations a scientific and structured approach to the problem of defining the relative worth of jobs is taken by methods collectively known as *job evaluation*.

Job Evaluation
"A generic term covering methods of determining the relative worth of jobs"

British Standards Institution
A1001

Why should some jobs be worth more than others?

Most people have strong feelings about which types of work are more important or prestigious than others. They may feel that being a doctor is more important than serving behind a bar, or that the managing director should be paid more than the cleaner. The question we have to ask is what is the source from which people make these judgements. We need to know whether there are any generally recognised standards which can be used to rank jobs in order of importance, worth, status and financial rewards.

The starting point is the feeling which most people have that things should be just and fair when it comes to status and rewards. We can define justice "as treating equals equally and unequals differently." This means that for jobs carrying similar responsibilities, all other things being equal, the gradings and rewards should be similar, while those people in less responsible positions should have lower gradings and smaller rewards.

Does this conform to your own idea of fairness — should a person receive a higher grade and a large salary for a more responsible and demanding job?

The responsibility involved in a job is not the only criterion for treating jobs differently. Listed below are a number of other factors which often lead to differences in grading and pay:

- The level of skill required.
- The pleasantness or unpleasantness of the work.
- The degree of danger in the work.
- The number of people being supervised.
- The amount of education and training required for the post.
- The amount of prior knowledge and/or experience required for the post.
- The degree of responsibility involved in the post.
- The degree of expertise needed to carry out the job.
- The shortage of a particular type of labour.
- The degree of job security in the post.

The problem which arises in large organisations, in particular, is how to put general notions of fairness and justice into action, and what degree of compensation to give for such things as additional responsibility or dangerous work. In over half of the big companies in Britain (those employing more than 5000 employees) this task is taken on by employing a method of *JOB EVALUATION*.

The Job not the Job Holder
Job Evaluation focuses on the job not the job holder. It is important to make a clear distinction between job evaluation and staff appraisal. The latter is a means of evaluating how well an individual has done in a job. Job evaluation by contrast, establishes what a job is and how it fits into the total organisational structure.

Activity: 'Job evaluation'

Before we investigate how job evaluation operates, let us analyse two jobs and make some comparisons between them — for argument's sake let us call them JOB A and JOB B. We will assume that they are located within the same company. Without any prior knowledge of *job evaluation* techniques you should read the job specifications and decide which is the more senior post. It is important for you to give reasons for the conclusions you come to.

JOB A	JOB B
Job title: Office Manager	*Job title*: Word Processing Supervisor
Accountability: To the Managing Director	*Accountability*: To the Office Manager
Staff Reporting: Four Office Supervisors	*Staff Reporting*: Five operators
Main Purpose: To ensure that the Office Services Division operates in the most efficient and effective fashion	*Main Purpose*: To ensure that word processing services of the Office Services Division are carried out in the most efficient fashion
Responsibilities	*Responsibilities*
1. To interview and recruit suitable staff	1. To supervise the word processing operators, and to make certain that all have sufficient work in accordance with their abilities
2. To ensure that the overall standards of performance are maintained	2. To train new operators when required, and to ensure that all existing staff have the necessary updating training
3. To hold regular meetings of the office supervisors to ensure co-ordination between the Sections of the Division and to produce weekly work schedules	3. To answer and check the work produced by the operators and to ensure that it conforms to company standards
4. To maintain regular contact with the Heads of other Divisions to ensure that the Office Service Division provides an effective service	4. To assist the operators with any difficulties and problems they encounter with equipment, software and layouts

5. To purchase new equipment and supplies	5. To organise the maintainence of equipment
6. To control the budget of the Division and prepare estimates	6. To keep up to date with changes in equipment and software packages
7. To ensure that all systems and procedures work efficiently and effectively	7. To liaise with other office supervisors when work requires services from other sections
8. To produce forward plans for the development of the Division after consulting other Divisions	8. To order all necessary stationery and equipment
9. To hold annual appraisal interviews with all staff in the Department	9. To carry out word processing functions when not carrying out supervisory functions
10. To advise the Personnel Division on staff business, upgradings and salary increases	10. To report on any significant deviations from the weekly work schedules to the Office Manager

Methods of job evaluation

There are a variety of different methods of ranking jobs. All of them have a number of common features and approaches. Before discussing the individual methods we shall discuss the factors they have in common. All schemes of job evaluation require some element of the following:

A thorough assessment of the job. The question must be asked 'what does this job entail?' We need to know such things as 'what are the responsibilities associated with it?', 'how many people, if any, are being supervised?' 'who does the post holder report to?'

The preparation of a job description. This is simply a written description of the important features of the job. Some methods of job evaluation require elaborate and detailed analysis of the post while for others a broad outline of responsibilities is sufficient. The job description will normally contain the job title, the accountability of the post holder and the nature of the responsibilities and duties associated with the post.

The comparison of one job with another to discover the relative worth of posts, or the comparing of one job with an established set of criteria.

Arranging or ranking jobs in an order of progression. An organisation will build up a hierarchy of posts or scales by evaluation, or will fit jobs into an existing hierarchy of scales.

The relating of jobs to a money or payments scale. It is important to establish a fair payments system related to the worth and content of jobs. A scheme of job evaluation enables this process to be carried out.

Job ranking

This is often called the *WHOLE JOB METHOD* of evaluation. In essence it is a method whereby the job as a whole is ranked in order of importance against other jobs. The ranking procedure is usually carried out by a panel of evaluators. It is a simple and straightforward method and seeks to answer the question — 'Is this job worthy of a higher grade than this other job?'

Activity: 'Job ranking'

Working with others in a group, rank the following occupations in order of importance.

NURSE
FIREFIGHTER
REFUSE COLLECTOR
PRIME MINISTER
DOCTOR
BANK MANAGER
SALESPERSON
SCIENTIST
FACTORY WORKER
TEACHER
GARDENER
LORRY DRIVER
FACTORY MANAGER

There is no one right answer to this activity. You can expect to have disagreements as your ranking will be affected by your own values and prejudices.

You might try to work out a set of criteria for rankings. These could be based on such factors as responsibilities, education, skills and training, although you may wish to enter other categories.

Job ranking is simple to understand and easy to operate, but it is also very subjective as you will see if you do the activity in this section. For this reason the results of ranking are often open to criticism.

You will also have noticed that this method only tells you about the degree of difficulty involved in each job and does not provide a detailed analysis of job content. This allows for a quick and simple comparison of jobs but lacks sophistication. Job ranking is a suitable method for small businesses but its lack of subtlety means that larger organisations require a more discriminating method.

Paired comparisons

A variation on job ranking is known as the *PAIRED COMPARISON METHOD*. This is a more sophisticated method of ranking. Like the job ranking system, jobs as a whole are compared by a panel of evaluators. In this method a sample of jobs between twenty-three and forty-three in number are compared. Each job is evaluated against every other job in the sample. Jobs are given a point score of 0, 1 or 2 depending on their importance. This enables every job to be compared with every other. The total points a job receives are totalled and from this a ranking is obtained.

Analytical methods

Analytical schemes break jobs down into elements or factors and each element is evaluated separately. One such method is the *POINTS RAT-ING SYSTEM*. In this system a job description is prepared for each post which carefully describes the following:

- The Job Title and where the job is located and performed.
- The physical conditions of the work — the duties involved, the working conditions and any equipment operating involved.
- The responsibilities and duties of the post together with such things as the degree of supervision, quality and standards of performance.

A panel of evaluators awards points for each factor according to a pre-determined scale and the total points awarded decide a job's place in the ranking order. Usually, the factors are weighted to reflect the varying degrees of importance attached to them. For example, if staff supervision is considered to be twice as important as responsibility for security, then it will be given a weighting twice that of the security factor. Care must be taken to ensure that the factor weightings do not result in a sex-biased scheme by, for example, attaching an unjustified weighting to a factor of physical strength at the expense of manual dexterity.

Typical factors into which posts can be divided include:

PERSONAL CONTACTS MADE BY THE POSTHOLDER
DURING THE COURSE OF HIS OR HER WORK
THE DEGREE OF CREATIVITY IN JOB
THE LEVEL OF DECISION-MAKING
TYPES OF DECISIONS MADE
SUPERVISORY RESPONSIBILITIES
SUPERVISION RECEIVED
THE COMPLEXITY OF THE WORK
THE AMOUNT OF EDUCATION AND TRAINING REQUIRED
FOR THE JOB
EXPERIENCE REQUIRED FOR THE JOB

Each of these factors is then broken down into a number of levels as is shown in the following example. Each level has a number of points associated with it. The points for the appropriate level on each factor are totalled and each job is given a score. This is then compared with a pre-determined list which shows the grade of post associated with each score.

An example of how points are allocated on a points rating scheme of job evaluation

Points		Decisions
10	Level 1	Few, if any, decisions are taken in the course of routine work
20	Level 2	Decisions of a largely routine nature
30	Level 3	Judgement is exercised between a limited number of alternatives
40	Level 4	Occasional decisions are taken which lead to minor changes of procedure
50	Level 5	Difficult decisions are taken which may change procedures affecting others
60	Level 6	Policy changes are taken which affect the direction of the organisation

A method such as points rating is complex and time consuming. By and large it is an objective and fair system as it breaks a job down into its constituent parts and then analyses them, but it is also a time-consuming procedure. In some large organisations the process of evaluating or re-evaluating a particular job may take between a year and eighteen months.

The great advantage of analytical methods over other methods of job evaluation is that it is relatively easy to explain to a post holder exactly why his or her job was or was not regraded. Precise levels on a range of factors can be cited as evidence. But like all methods, it has drawbacks and its success depends on the professionalism of the analysts. The use of numbers provides an appearance of precision and objectivity, but the process of locating factors depends entirely upon the skill of the analysts.

Job evaluation procedure under points rating

The following is a typical procedure which an organisation might adopt if it operated a points rating system of job evaluation.

1. At the start of the procedure a meeting of staff would be convened to explain the system and to give them an opportunity to discuss the evaluation with the analysts. The purpose of the exercise and the role the staff are expected to play in it will be explained. If it is a new scheme, there is usually protection given to individual post holders whose jobs are subsequently identified as over-graded.
2. All staff complete a job questionnaire which details the duties and responsibilities of their jobs and the time they spend on various duties and tasks.
3. The analysts use the questionnaire to hold interviews with each member of staff and with their immediate supervisors.
4. On the basis of the questionnaire and the interviews, the analysts draw up a detailed job description for each post. The job description is shown to the post holder who then signs it if it is acceptable. Disagreements may arise at this stage and require resolution.
5. A job evaluation panel is convened and from the job descriptions it decides on the appropriate level for each factor for particular jobs. Ideally, a panel will work by arriving at a consensus rather than by voting.
6. The points for the levels agreed by the panel are totalled and the score is compared with a pre-determined table showing the points for each grade. A post is located at the appropriate point of a scale for its score.
7. Where individuals feel that the panel has come to the wrong conclusion, they can usually appeal and a new panel is convened with more

senior management staff in attendance. The panel uses the same job description as the original panel and either confirms or alters the previous assessment. A re-assessment may be a downward assessment as well as an upward one.

Appeals are often the result of people not fully understanding the difference between job evaluation and staff appraisal. A person may have a very routine job with few opportunities for creativity, but because of hard work and force of personality may have a reputation for diligence and effectiveness which is out of the ordinary. Job evaluation does not deal with this and a person may feel aggrieved that hard work is going unrecognised. Job evaluation does not concern itself with individual performance, only with the ranking of the job. It is through staff appraisal that an individual's efforts can be recognised and, perhaps, rewarded.

Criticisms of job evaluation

The growth of job evaluation has not been without its critics who argue that while it has solved problems it has done so only by creating others.

The first criticism is that job evaluation does not allow for the reward of merit and performance. If two posts are evaluated as being on the same scale, then their post holders will receive the same salary regardless of how well they perform their functions.

The second criticism is that job evaluation does not take into account market forces. Organisations which have strictly evaluated grading structures can find it difficult to fill certain vacancies or recruit suitable staff in areas where there is a labour shortage. This is particularly the case with computer staff. A firm which does not use job evaluation will merely adjust the gradings and the pay in order to recruit the staff it requires. Job evaluation can be a hindrance to adjusting to particular shortages in the labour market.

Geographical factors are not considered when evaluating posts but the wide differential in house prices, living conditions and labour availability in different parts of the country might suggest that this should be reflected in levels of pay.

This view was summed up by the then Paymaster-General, Mr Kenneth Clarke, in a speech in 1987 at the City University when he said,

"Why should a music teacher in Inverness earn the same as a maths teacher in Surrey . . . I see no reason why bank clerks, civil servants, and teachers are paid the same irrespective of who they work for and in which part of the country they live in . . . An efficient and effective labour market would respond with different rates of pay for companies, industries and geographical areas." (Quoted in the *Times Educational Supplement*, 20th February 1987)

There are two conflicting ideas of fairness in payments and grading systems. The first on which job evaluation is based is that everybody doing the same work should be paid and graded the same, and that there should be rational and defensible criteria for deciding differences in grading and pay.

The other concept of fairness is based on market forces. The argument is that individual merit and performance is what ought to be rewarded and not a notional job description. It is seen as unfair for a good and a poor employee to receive the same salary merely because they have the same paper responsibilities. Neither is it thought to be just that people should be paid the same regardless of whether they live in a high or a low cost region.

A method of attempting a reconciliation of these two notions of fairness is to use job evaluation systems which are more flexible and responsive to individual performance and market forces. This can involve market force payments for shortage skill areas, merit payments for high individual performance, and regional supplements in areas of high cost housing.

SECTION IV

PEOPLE

CHAPTER 20

Groups

One of the major features of a BTEC course is that much of the work is carried out in groups. BTEC encourages this form of working because it is in groups, both formal and informal, that people spend much of their time at work. Those of you who are part-time students will have already experienced this and know the importance of working with others to the success of an enterprise. In fact, the individual method of working still employed by many secondary schools is a rather exceptional activity. In most spheres of life we do things by working in concert with others.

> *An important idea in business is SYNERGY. You will have experienced it while working in well-run groups. The amount of energy, enthusiasm and ideas generated by a group is often more than the sum of the ideas and energy of the individuals who make it up. Good teams work in exciting and creative ways.*

You cannot learn to be a good team member by reading a book. You will learn group work skills by working in groups, but you can be helped to reflect on your experiences. Such reflection can be a guide to establishing a better working relationship with colleagues.

Groups vary enormously, and range from formal work groups such as committees to *ad hoc*, informal social groups. They can produce creative and imaginative work or they can waste people's time. They can be a source of satisfaction to their members, but they often are the cause of frustration.

What is a group?

Are a number of people waiting at a railway station a group?
Do shoppers queueing at the supermarket checkout constitute a group?

167

When did your course cease to be a collection of individuals and become a group?

We need to analyse the difference between a number of isolated individuals in close proximity, such as those waiting for a train, and groups. Groups have special characteristics or identities. It is important to ask how they acquire them. What was it that turned the members of your course into a group? Was it the fact of knowing each other's names or was it some early experience which you all shared, perhaps joining for coffee in the canteen, which shaped you as a group?

We suspect that one of the most important shared experiences for your course members was the fact that you were all new in the College together. Helping each other to come to terms with new places and faces and different ways of working draws people to each other. Bonds are formed, and are then strengthened by further common experiences. Usually, the more difficult or traumatic the situation, the stronger the bonds which tie the group together. A disaster or an unpleasant or dangerous occurrence unites people in ways which would be unthinkable in ordinary circumstances.

What makes a group a group?

Aims: Any group shares common goals and aims. A group must have a purpose. It could be friendship, fly fishing, football or freefall parachuting. The existence of aims are important because to achieve them the group must pull together.

Identity   All groups take on an identity. It is this quality which makes the group different and separate from the rest of the world. Group members know they belong, and their collective identity may be signalled in a special form of dress or language.

Membership: For a group to be a group it must have at least two members.

Structures: All groups have at least a minimum of structure. They must meet together and there is usually a dominant personality and leader. In general, the larger the group, the more complex the structure of the group.

Activity: 'Group membership'

1. List the groups of which you are a member.
2. What features can you identify which are common to all the groups?
3. What is the main purpose or aim of each of these groups — for example, work related, social, family, etc.
4. How did you become a member of each of these groups?
5. Try to identify with those aspects of group membership which give you satisfaction and those aspects which cause frustration.

Formal and informal groups

Groups can be divided into formal and informal categories.

Formal — are groups set up to achieve a defined purpose. They have officers or persons with formal and specific roles, and record their proceedings and decisions. Formal groups usually have a degree of permanence.

Informal — are social groups where the roles are defined through the interplay of personalities. Such groups may have definite purposes — cycling or drinking beer — but their aims are usually defined through social interaction, not through formal decision-making. Social and informal groups can and do operate in the work place and they can become very powerful. Cabals and secret societies have always been an effective means of influence and achieving power. Often informal groups have a temporary or transient existence.

What are groups good at?

Problem-solving — groups can be very effective at solving problems as they pool views and perspectives.

Decision-making — participation in decision-making means that group members are more inclined to be committed to decisions than if decisions are taken by others.

Allocating work — groups can allocate work according to the ability of their members.

Co-ordination and liaison — group activity is an effective way of distributing tasks between functions and departments.

Participation and involvement — group work allows individuals to become involved with the work of organisations.

Negotiation and conflict resolution	— group pressures are a useful vehicle for resolving conflicts and for negotiating difficult problems.
Evaluation	— group work can be a valuable means of evaluating and monitoring the success of past activities.
Information processing and gathering	— groups, through their communication network, provide a useful means of intelligence gathering and documentation.
Brainstorming and generating ideas	— one of the most effective uses of group work is in the generation of ideas.

Group norms

One of the major features of any group is that it develops its own *norms* of behaviour. These are conscious or subconscious patterns of behaviour, values and ways of operating which are particular and peculiar to each individual group. Group norms are the badge or uniform which marks a group out as a distinct entity. All groups develop in this way to some extent. For some, the norms are subtle and are barely perceptible, while for others dress, speech and behaviour are self-consciously different and are designed to set the group apart.

Group norms are the 'cement' which holds the group together. They give the group an identity. The strength of a group to unleash new ideas can only be established if it has first decided on its own values and rules of operation.

Some examples of group norms are listed below:

distinctive gestures and mannerisms
ways of speaking and 'in-words'
dress
formality and informality
degree of participation
method of procedure

Group norms help to bind a group together, and they are particularly useful during periods of tension or strain. In fact, many norms have their origin in time of crisis where the adoption of a particular form of behaviour saved the situation. Norms are dynamic and constantly changing. This is especially the case where other groups try to copy another's pattern of behaviour. To preserve its special identity, a group will adopt new ways of maintaining its separateness.

Initiation into a group involves observing the norms of that group. Introduce a new member on to a committee or into a team and until the other members are certain of the newcomer's loyalty he or she will remain an outsider. The exclusion may be subtle or explicit but group members practise it until they can be certain that the new person is ready for full membership. Some groups may have formal procedures of initiation for newcomers into full membership.

Stages of group development

We must never think of groups as static entities. All groups grow, develop, change and eventually die. A successful marketing team can run out of ideas, while a struggling football team can be taken to heights of undreamed of success by the appointment of a new manager. Groups have a life of their own and consequently they have a life cycle. To make a group work you need to realise this. You cannot put four or five people into a room and expect a fully mature and operational group to be formed in half an hour. A group must learn to grow. What we will explore here is the life cycle of a group.

Forming

Groups do not start off by having an identity. Initially, they are no more than collections of individuals who come together for a purpose and they have to be formed into a group. This stage is characterised by discussion about what the group is going to do, what its aims are, what rules its members will take and what its terms of reference are. It is in this stage that particular individuals attempt to make an impression upon the group.

Storming

This is a normal stage, but one that disturbs many groups and group members, and one that some groups never recover from because they fail to recognise it as normal. It may be characterised by a leadership crisis, a challenge to the terms of reference or by individuals seeking to plant their personal agendas on the process. The storming stage is important as it tests the loyalty of the members of the group to its aims. To become mature, a group must be able to resolve conflicts within its ranks.

Norming

A group has to have its own set of values, known as norms. These are the practices by which it works and makes decisions. The norming processes establish the identity of a group. It is at this stage that important issues such as the style of leadership and the methods of working are decided.

Performing

This is the stage during which the mature group undertakes productive tasks. Some work may have been carried out during previous stages but it is now that the real work is done. Of course, a crisis can blow up at any time but if the previous stages have been properly managed, then the group has means of overcoming crises. In a mature group, this stage will make up most of the life of the group.

Some groups never reach this stage and collapse because they have failed to establish an identity, goals and a structure.

Features of an effective work group

An effective work group has a number of characteristics. They can be categorised as follows.

Clarity of objectives

Groups tackle tasks best when their objectives are clear.

Ambiguity in a task can lead to a great deal of time being spent on definition and not on performance. If this is the case, then the storming and norming stages may be unnecessarily prolonged. A creative work group requires clear terms of reference.

Performance criteria

How does a group know when it is doing well? A measure of effectiveness can help it achieve goals and provide a means of self-checking so that a work group can measure whether it is on course. If a group is asked to look at cost saving operations, then it will need to know what level of savings can be regarded as a successful achievement.

Commitment and trust

The more commitment group members have to their task, the higher the performance that can be expected from each member. Trust among members is important as it reduces the power of 'hidden agendas' and encourages members to be more open about their feelings.

Leadership

This is crucial to the health of the group. The actual style of leadership is less important than its existence or influence. While single leaders are the norm, leadership can be exercised by any group member. In a crisis or moment of doubt, any group member can raise morale or take on the task of strengthening the group's resolve. Leadership is not a prerogative of management, but a manager in charge of a group will be expected to exercise the function of leadership.

Procedures

An effective group has clear and well-understood procedures to work by. A group has to know how decisions are made so that any individual member knows how to influence a decision. The processes of recording decisions and reporting on actions taken are crucial features of the effective group.

Environment and assistance

Work groups need support from management, other groups and fellow workers.

A hostile environment will cause a group to spend much of its time working for its survival rather than tackling the tasks on hand.

Behaviour in groups

If groups are to be effective, then group members need to develop roles which enable them to act in flexible ways and to adjust their roles to meet changing situations. There are a range of behaviours which can assist task achievement in groups:

Suggesting: creating new ideas to solve a group's problems.
Building: adding to proposals already made in order to improve their quality.
Clarifying: groups often find that from time to time they become diverted from their original task. Objectives need to be clarified.
Informing: all groups need relevant and useful information.
Summarising: bringing together ideas and presenting them in a coherent fashion.

Supporting: it is important that good ideas receive a warm, friendly
                and supportive response from group members. This en-
                courages a climate in which new ideas can bloom.
Reconciling: bringing together differences of view especially if they
                could lead to conflict.
Listening: other people's ideas need an audience. Listening is one of
                the most important functions that people can perform for
                each other.

Group roles

In groups, each individual takes on a special role or set of roles which
marks him or her out as different from everyone else in the group.
Sometimes an individual consciously decides to become the 'investigator'
or 'leader' or 'joker', but it is also the case that the group may *label* its
members. The group may decide that a member is the 'peacemaker' or the
'supporter'. Labelling can also be used to isolate a member by blaming him
or her for all that goes wrong. This is called *scapegoating*.

The following are some typical group roles. You may want to attach your
own labels and add some categories of your own.

Leader	Supporter	Withdrawer
Follower	Investigator	Passifier
Joker	Outsider	Peacemaker
Dominator	Ideas-person	Organiser
Aggressor	Special-interest pleader	Proposer
Innovator		Scapegoat

You will notice that some of these roles are useful for the maintenance and
health of the group, while others are adopted for the ego-needs of
particular individuals. A 'dominator' is usually a selfish role whereas a
'supporter' or an 'investigator' is an asset to the group.

Some roles are said to be *functional* (that is, useful for group maintenance), whereas others are *dysfunctional*. The dysfunctional roles are
irrelevant to the group and may actually be prejudicial to its operation.
Groups need to be self-conscious and aware of the roles its members are
adopting. Too many members adopting dysfunctional roles can spell the
end to the group as a useful and harmonious entity.

Roles can also be categorised into:

Task roles and
Maintenance roles

Task roles are those which are useful for achieving things:

Leading
Proposing new courses of action
Building
Seeking new information
Summarising

Maintenance roles are those which help to maintain group solidarity:

Releasing tension
Giving attention
Gatekeeping (deciding who to let in and who to keep out)
Supporting
Encouraging

Interactions in groups

Interactions between members of groups take place in a variety of ways depending upon the nature and style of the leadership in the group. The interactions between the members are often portrayed as being of three types characterised by models known as the wheel, the circle and fully interactional.

The wheel

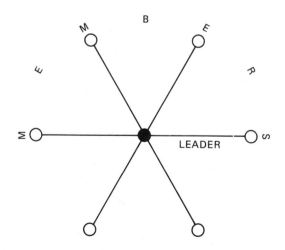

The wheel is used to describe the decision-making process in a group dominated by a leader. The leader may ask group members for their opinion and then assess the quality of their responses. As ordinary members have little interactions with each other, it is a fast method of decision-making. The problem is that ordinary members may feel isolated in the process. The effectiveness of the group depends upon the effectiveness of the leader.

The circle

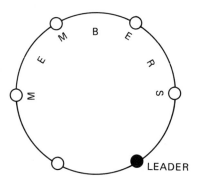

The circle is a slow and cumbersome method of making decisions as it is necessary for the leader to consult each member in turn.

Fully interactional

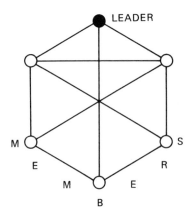

The fully interactional model is a useful one to follow for effective decision-making. If time permits, then all members can have the opportunity to participate. It provides members with a strong sense of group commitment. However, it may take the group a long time to reach decisions.

Quality circles

A quality circle is a small group of employees who meet together voluntarily for an hour or so a week. Led by their supervisor they discuss, analyse and solve problems connected with their jobs. It is a concept which originated in Japan and has been copied by many European companies who have looked to follow Japanese success, much of which has been built around the quality of their products.

Quality is used in a very broad sense and discussions can involve any matter connected with the product or service which affects the efficiency of the work place. Health and safety matters, new procedures and the diagnosis of faults are all legitimate matters of concern in addition to the physical quality of the product.

The idea is a very simple one and at first sight it is perhaps difficult to see why so many companies are enthusiastic about promoting the operation of quality circles. The reason has to do with attitudes to work and the power of groups to motivate and to solve problems.

Companies which operate quality circles acknowledge the enormous benefits which group working can bring. But they have to adopt new management styles and practices to accommodate them. Management has to share its prerogative with its work force and to allow them to participate in the decision-making process. Employees who take part in quality circles demonstrate an interest and concern for wealth creation and in the nature of the work they do.

There are a number of benefits to the company. From the management side, there are clear gains in both improved industrial relations and a more efficient organisation. It finds that its workforce is more committed and willing to put their own time into improving products. In return for these gains, management has to be prepared to share policy decisions with its employees and to derive new participatory styles of managing.

The employees benefit because work takes on a new interest. The process of group working is stimulating and the process of problem solving adds a new dimension to work. Quality circles are a source of motivation and job satisfaction.

Those companies who have employed the quality circle idea have discovered that, given the right atmosphere, employees want to contribute to the running of the organisation. The operational efficiency improves and people feel a greater sense of involvement with their jobs. Quality circles are one practical way in which the dynamics of groups can be utilised in a business setting.

Activity: 'Analysing a work group'

In this activity, well-established work groups should analyse their own workings. The activity will work best if the group focuses on its last performance, say a group assignment.
  The group should analyse:

Its group norms
  What are they?
  How were they established?
  What function do they perform?
The roles within the group
  How did the roles first come to be allocated?
  What roles do members play?
  Are any of the roles dysfunctional?
  Distinguish between task and maintenance roles in the group. Is the balance between them right?

Discuss how successful your group has been at performing tasks. You can use the observation checklist which follows to help you in this.

Group observation checklist

  Did the group have clear aims?
  Did the group immediately set about its appointed task?
  Was there a commitment to the group by its members?
  Did any particular member(s) of the group withdraw from
    the proceedings?
  Were there any disagreements over the course of action to
    be taken?
  How were disagreements resolved?
  How were decisions taken?
  Were decisions fully supported?
  Were the resources of the group fully utilised?
  Did meetings keep to their agendas?
  How effectively was the time for group meetings used?
  Was the atmosphere conducive to task fulfilment?
  What was the quality of leadership like?

Were all the feelings of group members fully expressed?
Other comments.

CHAPTER 21

Self-presentation

We all have an image of ourselves. Our self-image influences our behaviour and it affects the way in which we present ourselves to others.

In order to understand your self-presentation, you need to be certain of your identity. You may already have a clear idea that you are 'the strong, silent type' or 'the life and soul of the party', but are you right?

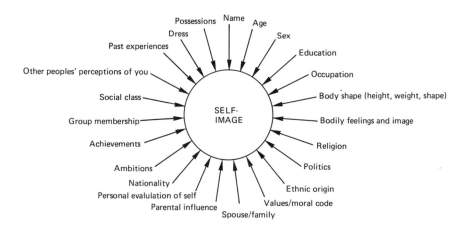

Figure 35   A personal image map

You must, however, be careful not to be carried away by fantasy; if you see yourself as the managing director when clearly you are not, then no amount of positive thinking can change things. You must have your own self-image tempered by reality and by other people's perception of you.

Our self-image is formed through the reactions of others. We come to see ourselves as others see us. This reflection of ourselves in the reaction of others is sometimes called 'the looking glass self'. People compare themselves physically — "I must be very short because all my friends are taller than I am"; with the success of others — "I am not very successful because my friends have more/better qualifications than I have"; and particularly in terms of possessions — "why can't I afford the new outfit/holiday/car, etc., that others can?" Who do you compare yourself with? Do you consciously have reference points, groups and people against whom you measure yourself? If you do, are they *realistic* references? Many people have a low opinion of themselves because they are unrealistic in their references. A better way forward is to be yourself. Set yourself realistic goals and then compare what you do against them.

Roles

We all have roles which we play out. Some, like our sex, are assigned to us. We do not choose to be male or female, to be a son or a daughter, or to be an orphan or a member of a large family, but these roles shape our personality. If we are given the role of girl/woman and we choose to marry then we are assigned the role of wife. Other roles we choose. While writing this book we were authors. You when reading this book will be in the role of student. But these roles are not exclusive; there are hosts of other roles which we can play. Those of you in employment will have your work roles, which are among the most important roles you will fill. When people first meet you, they often ask 'what do you do?' You may answer 'shop assistant, bank clerk, driving instructor . . . '. The roles we take on, office or shop-worker, youth-club leader, company-director, form a distinctive aspect of our personality.

> *Do you conform to the stereotype for your work role? Is your role part of your personality, or do you wear a mask?*

Of course, some people have a much stronger sense of identity than others. There are people who may be uncertain about who they are and experience crises of identity at various periods in their lives. For example, school or college leavers starting a new job may face an identity crisis. Not only are they leaving the familiarity of daily routine and friendships, but they will be discovering new challenges, meeting new people and experiencing new situations. For those young people unable to find employment, the situation can be even more threatening; a life away from one's friends and familiar surroundings and routines can be lonely and depressing.

The subject of personal identity is important for your work, and it is important for the people you work with. The way you feel about yourself and the way you feel about how others regard you is a major influence on your happiness, and on your mental attitude. Your work performance is directly related to the state of your self-assurance. In chapter 22 on Motivation you will discover, what you may already know, that people do not work just for money. People have a wide range of wants and needs which have to be satisfied. One of the most important of these needs is that of self-esteem. If you do not feel that you are valued at work, then you will not feel satisfied with your job. The people you work with may feel the same way; perhaps you can make the difference for them? It is not only 'the boss' who can show that staff are valued. Colleague can value colleague, subordinate can value superior, and so on. Do you show that you value other people? If a colleague has a work problem, do you listen? If another colleague wants to share his or her pride in some achievement, will you give your time for them? We all have opportunities to show that we value other people and care about what they are and what they do.

How should I put my message across?

Self-presentation has a good deal to do with communication. If I stand up in front of an audience looking dishevelled and shabby and mumble then, however good the information, my message may well be lost. If the medium is the message, then we must look right and sound right for the audience. Part of our image to others is transmitted through appearance:

- hair
- clothes
- posture
- voice
- style of behaviour

These features signal things to others about our seriousness or lack of it, our reliability, intelligence, honesty and our care and concern for them. When people see us dress or act in particular ways they expect certain things of us. Some people are often surprised by the way in which total strangers place trust in them. The reason is that they are people who look and sound trustworthy. To say that these non-verbal features of communications do not matter is to misunderstand how people react. It may be that people should not 'judge a book by its cover', but at a first meeting it is the case that impressions count.

But, of course, 'looks can be deceiving' and non-verbal symbols can mislead and can sometimes be designed to do so. The 'con-artist' operates in just this way, taking people in by giving an impression to disguise his or her real intention. Deception and concealment are common — not all of it is malicious. Many people conceal embarrassment or fear with a 'front'. Often a confident look is a means of hiding an uncertain personality.

How far should we go? Should we always be totally sincere and never put on a front? Should we say to our boss I cannot do this because I am shy, or should we fight the shyness, put on a brave face and be congratulated afterwards for being so confident? The answer is difficult. One should never deceive others, lie or conceal the truth. However, learning a role often means 'wearing a mask' which may mean not being ourselves for that learning period. If we do this we need to be certain that the role we are hoping to grow into is one we want, can cope with, and one that adds to the sum of human happiness.

Yourself and others

One of the most important aspects of your business life is the manner in which you deal with other people. Whether you are employed in sales, banking, the public service or retailing, and regardless of your organisation's size, the interactions with your colleagues, customers and clients are crucial both for your enjoyment of your work and for the performance of the business.

'Gate Keepers'
You may say, 'but I am too junior to have any effect on the performance and fortunes of the organisation'. That statement is untrue. It is often the case in business that the people in the front line who deal directly with the public are young or relatively junior or both. Receptionists, bank and building society cashiers, and sales assistants are among the people the customer meets first. It is the quality of the service and the way they are treated by these **gate keepers** *that determines their attitude to the business.*

Everyday of our working lives we have contacts with scores of other people. Most of these exchanges are fleeting and consist of recognition symbols — smiles, nods, waves and eye contacts. They pass virtually unnoticed and are retained only in our short-term memory. We also have dealings with other people of quite a different magnitude. There are meetings and relationships which are important to us and to the people we interact with. Contacts with family, friends and colleagues at work and at college come into this category. From time to time, we experience encounters which are significant to our view of the world and which may shape our personality and our future. We all remember the first meeting with a boy or girl friend or a significant appraisal interview.

It is important for your working life that you make a success of your contacts with others. Business is about meeting other people's wishes and needs, and a business which does not meet this objective will fail. Personal skills, just like any other skill, can be acquired and improved upon. Your performance will require reflection and self-evaluation. This is particularly the case where the interactions are difficult or unfamiliar. Many people when first promoted to supervisory roles find it difficult to give instructions to others; while others find arguing their case with a more senior colleague a daunting prospect. There is no single method of dealing with difficult and stressful encounters, but practice and reflection are necessary to improve performance.

Some guidelines for personal contacts at work

Always be polite. It is important always to greet people when you meet them and to use 'please' and 'thank you'. As important as being polite is being sincere. There is no point in saying 'thank you' unless you mean it. *Display the proper degree of formality.* Customers and clients are greeted by a firm handshake. They are addressed as Mr, Mrs or Miss until you know them well enough to be on first name terms. It is up to the clients to extend the invitation to use their first name.

Be interested in what is being said to you. To the customer you are the organisation. If you are not interested in the customer's needs then there is a good chance that they will take their business elsewhere. Maintaining eye contact is important to showing interest.

Never argue with customers. The old adage 'the customer is always right' is largely correct. Unless you can satisfy the demands of your customers, the organisation will go out of business and you will have no livelihood. Customers, in reality, are often wrong. You should inform them when they are, but do *not* argue with them. Arguments force people into corners and make them defend their views. There is a time and place to argue, but when dealing with customers it is your job to persuade them. The best way to do this is always to be certain of your facts.

Look good and be smart. Your appearance is important, and this takes us back to an earlier point we made about first impressions. To the customers you represent the organisation. People who care about their appearance give the impression that they care about the customer.

Stand up when customers and clients enter your room or approach your desk. Never greet people sitting down, as it is the height of rudeness. When people meet you: stand up, shake them by the hand and offer them a seat.

Avoid keeping people waiting. Always put the customer first. If a customer has come to see you, then you have to make him or her your priority. If you cannot see visitors immediately, make certain you apologise to them, make them comfortable, find them something to read and give them a cup of coffee if their wait is to be prolonged. Tell them how long they will have to wait and then keep to the deadline.

Take responsibility for your actions. When something goes wrong it is easy to put the blame on to others, or on outside forces. If you find yourself doing this ask the question 'was this my fault; did I cause this to happen?' If it was the fault of others — well fine, but be certain before exporting the blame.

It is important for you to take responsibility for your own actions. Everybody makes mistakes and it is from them that you will learn. If you cannot admit to mistakes, you will not be able to develop in your work.

In your relationships with others you need to display a confidence that you are certain about yourself and your actions. This confidence should stem from self-assurance that you and you alone are responsible for your actions and the consequences which flow from them.

Being assertive

We handle our personal relations best when we are sensitive to the needs of others and assertive in our manner. This is the adult way of dealing with other people. It is honest and it will allow you to express your ideas and feelings openly. If you are assertive, you will not be tempted to put down other people's ideas and feelings in order to establish your own.

Too many people's encounters are *COMPETITIVE*. They are based on trying to win points or gain an advantage over others. Competitive exchanges can leave people with negative feelings about their encounters. People who engage in competitive encounters may end up feeling bad about losing or guilty about winning. 'Winning' often involves manipulating others or using aggression to force others to accept a view.

While you should not use these tactics to get your own way, neither should you let others engage in them when dealing with you. Being assertive involves standing up for your rights and not feeling guilty about having done so. It is your right to express what you believe. You will find that taking this stand will give you the respect of other people.

It is often difficult to be assertive if it does not come naturally to you. A good starting point is to accept responsibility for your own actions, thoughts and ideas. If you do this then the next step is to be prepared to defend them if they come under threat. You should not engage in argument for its own sake. It is important to listen to the views of others and to be prepared to modify your own in the light of other points of view.

But in the last analysis, you must decide what you believe in and how you want to live your life.

The next step on the road to being assertive is not to feel guilty about things which are not your fault or your responsibility. You have to be responsible for yourself, but you cannot take responsibility for the actions of others and neither should you. You will come across people who try to manipulate others by trying to make them feel guilty about matters which are nothing to do with them. It is a common tactic and can be very effective, especially with very conscientious people. People can be made to feel very guilty about not doing what is not their job. The aim is to make them take on more work. Sometimes the manipulation is subtle and can involve group pressure. You may have experienced this and felt guilty for not staying late, working through your lunch hour or not taking work home.

In order to be assertive, you must learn to say no. It is often difficult to say because of the response it evokes in others. If you do say no you may find that you will have to deal with anger, frustration, manipulation, pressure, sorrow or rejection. For this reason many people say yes when they mean no and end up feeling sad, hurt and manipulated. We have said earlier that you must take responsibility for yourself. You have a right to say no. If a friend offers drugs and you do not want them, say no. There is no obligation to give an explanation. It is up to you to decide if you want to give an explanation of your behaviour, but people who make offers have no rights to explanations if you reject them. Saying no is an important part of assertive behaviour.

An important aspect is not to put the blame on to others for any negative responses you might make. Do not say no and then say 'I would really like to, but my parents will not let me', or 'I do not have any transport'. This is copping-out. If you mean no, then take responsibility for saying it.

Assertive behaviour allows a person to be able to deal in an adult manner with difficult situations. It allows you to make your case openly and positively without having to be aggressive or submissive.

Structuring arguments and persuading others

The world of business revolves around the effective presentation of ideas and views. Salespeople have to find means of interesting potential customers in the need to purchase their products. Negotiators have to persuade others of their case. Members of policy-making committees have to convince fellow members of the virtue of their proposals.

Persuading others is a key business skill. It is also an important aspect of the effectiveness of communication. 'Winning Friends and Influencing People' is perhaps a good slogan in this respect, but we need to be clear about what we are doing when we are trying to persuade others and the effect of our efforts on them and on us.

The use of the mass media by business is concerned largely with this one aspect of communications — persuasion. Advertising is about developing wants in people and then making those wants into needs which can only be satisfied by the purchase of particular goods and services.

How can we persuade others?

There are a considerable range of methods at our disposal for this purpose, and some are more legitimate in business than others.

The use of power

This is the least subtle of all means of persuasion. Quite simply, those with power can use force, threats, intimidation or the power that goes with their position, to persuade those without power to do what they want.

Of course, power can be used in more legitimate ways. It is often the case that many people respect the status of those in authority and are more likely to obey their requests than the requests of people who do not occupy such roles.

The use of expert knowledge

A powerful source of persuasion is that of expertise. People will take notice of the advice or instructions of an expert. It is easier for a doctor than a friend or relative to persuade a person to quit smoking.

The use of rational argument

People can be persuaded to change their minds, follow a line of thinking or a course of action, because they have been convinced of the validity of a case. Rational argument consists of cataloguing the facts into those for and against and then weighing up the evidence. Decisions are made by judging which course of action yields the greater benefit. The facts are allowed to speak for themselves.

The use of emotion

One of the most effective means of persuading others is to use emotion. Here the appeal is not to fact but to the feelings of another. It has two sides to it, a positive and a negative aspect.

On the negative side an appeal to emotion may take the form of a threat: 'you will feel guilty unless you do the following'; 'Imagine how you will feel if you do that'; 'please do not take that course of action because I will feel hurt if you do'. In these cases, emotional persuasion will be used to override another's rational judgement.

But appeals to emotion do have a very positive side. Charities and organisations appeal to our sense of compassion, love for others and desire to ease suffering. Our concern for others and our desire to do good for them — altruism — may override what may be seen as the best for our narrow, but rational, self-interest.

A person's feelings can be as good a guide for making decisions as rational judgement. Many business people rely on their intuition or the feel they have for a situation. It is probably true to say that intuitive judgements are less reliable than rational judgements. It is possible to have carefully weighed all the evidence and still to be wrong, but at least the decision would be taken on the best possible evidence and the chances of mistakes are minimised. Intuitive judgements can be disastrous, but equally they may also be brilliant.

The use of personal relationships

Many people use their relationships with others to influence them. The pressure may be subtle — playing on a friendship or family ties — or it can be blatant — by implying that affection will be increased or friendship withdrawn if a particular course of action is followed.

Doing other people favours can fall into this category. If favours are 'sold' so that another is beholden and has to provide favours in return, then personal relationships are being used in a manipulative way.

Are any means fair to persuade others?

From our discussion it can be seen that some forms of persuasion are more legitimate than others. Clearly, forcing people to do something against their will, lying to them or misusing authority should never be employed. Similarly, emotional extortion is not an adult way of trying to influence others.

Appeals to emotion can be perfectly legitimate but not if they involve threats — 'unless you do the following you will feel guilty'. Rational or expert arguments are also adult ways of making a case, provided that the facts are presented in a fair and unbiased fashion.

It is important to be aware of the possibility of *bias* which can exist in all argument and persuasion. However rational and objective we try to be we all have our own sets of values, views and beliefs which colour the way we see the world and influence what we say and do. We need to recognise the bias behind the views of others and the biases in our own presentations.

CHAPTER 22

Motivation and Human Needs

What makes people work hard and give of their best at work? Here are some typical answers. Which of them do you most readily relate to?

'I like to know that I have achieved something which others value'
'What motivates me is having my achievements recognised'
'I want to gain promotion and doing a good job is a means of achieving that'
'I get a kick out of solving problems'
'I enjoy earning the money and the bonuses that the job brings with it'

The subject of motivation is one of the most discussed topics in any company. Every organisation wants to employ keen, dedicated and hard-working employees who are able to improve performance. The problem is how can people with these qualities be employed and retained, and how can other employees who lack motivational qualities be encouraged to improve their performance.

This chapter has been written to help you think about your own motivation. It is designed to help you answer the question 'what motivates me?'

Motivation is linked with the satisfaction of needs and drives — feeling good, in non-technical language — and unless you understand what motivates you, then you may find yourself in the wrong job and the wrong career. If your source of motivation is money, then it would be a mistake to start a career as a nurse, a social worker or a teacher. If you gain satisfaction from being surrounded by people, then you need to choose an occupation which meets this need. Throughout this book we have been working on the theme that you must know yourself and what drives you. If you understand this, then you will be on the way to making suitable career choices.

What is motivation

Motivation is the drive we have to pursue goals. These may be personal ambitions for more money, a bigger car or house, power, status and other visible achievements. Or they might be organisational goals such as higher performance targets. People are said to be motivated when they freely pursue goals with energy and enthusiasm.

> *People are motivated when they want to do a good job, not because someone is threatening or bribing them.*

Human needs

To understand motivation, we need to understand the psychology of human needs. We need an insight into why people act as they do. We start from the proposition that people, unless they are being coerced, do what they like doing or, in other words, what gives them satisfaction and pleasure. Conversely, people avoid things which hurt them and give them pain and suffering. They do not voluntarily do things which they dislike. When acting in these ways, people are exhibiting *rational* behaviour or, to put it another way, they do things for reasons which make sense to them.

One reason why motivation is such a complex subject is that people are complex. They act in the ways they do because it satisfies a basic innate drive, for example, for food and drink, or because they wish to pursue goals which are the result of thought and reflection. Motivation is an aspect of personality and consequently the needs and drives of individuals are personal to them. This means that the features of a job which are stimulating and exciting to one person may not be so for another. For this reason, motivation will always be the key problem for any organisation, and the nature of the problem will alter as the personnel changes.

Activity: 'Motivation — a self analysis'

Do you find it easier to do things you like rather than those which you do not?
Do you feel a particular need for security?
Do you feel a particular need to belong to social groups?
Do you need other people to recognise your achievements? Is a pat on the back important to you?
What aspects of your work and study do you particularly enjoy?

In what ways can you make your work and study more interesting?
Have you discussed with your supervisor/tutor ways in which your job/study can be made more interesting?
What are your career ambitions?
What do you expect to be doing in a year from now?
What action will you be taking to reach your goals?

In any discussion of human motivation the theories of the American psychologist Abraham Maslow are always to the fore. Dr Maslow was born in New York in 1908 and died in 1970. In books such as *Motivation and Personality* (1954) he attempted to produce what is known as a universalistic theory of human nature. That is to say, a theory which applies to all people at all times and is not just limited to any individual or particular situations in business life. The aspects of Maslow's theory which particularly concern us are those aspects usually known as the 'hierarchy of human needs'.

Maslow's theory describes the instinctual needs common to all human beings. The key idea is that needs are *hierarchical*. This is to say that once a set of needs is satisfied then other needs start to become evident. Higher-order needs such as those for creativity and achievement do not become evident until more basic needs, such as those for shelter and food, are satisfied. No one cares about their status if they are starving to death. What Maslow's theory illustrates is that people are wanting beings whose needs, once they are satisfied, lead to the generation of new needs. Maslow's classification of need can be described as follows (see figure 36):

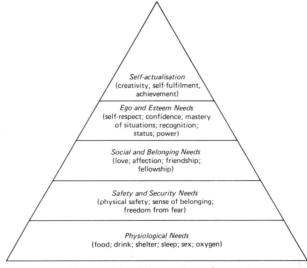

Figure 36 Hierarchy of needs

Physiological Needs

These are the most basic and most necessary for human survival — food, drink, sleep, sex, shelter and oxygen. Work usually allows these needs to be satisfied indirectly via the payment of money in the form of salary. In addition, some organisations go further by providing accommodation for their employees and/or subsidised canteens and other benefits.

Safety and Security Needs

These needs are based on a desire for certainty and of security from physical danger. Company policy is a major factor in satisfying this need, via such measures as sickness and pension schemes. A major cause of insecurity in the current economic climate is redundancy, and successful companies meet the security need by being able to guarantee employment to their workers.

Social and Belonging Needs

Human beings require love, affection, friendship and fellowship. At work, these needs can be satisfied informally via contacts with other employees or more formally through company social clubs, outings, etc. They are important needs and the most influential in providing a fulfilling work situation. Many people when asked what is the most satisfying feature of their job say 'the people I work with'.

Ego and Esteem Needs

These needs are of two types:

Self-esteem needs, which include the desire for competence, confidence, achievement, status and power.
Respect from others, which includes the need for acceptance, reputation, prestige and appreciation.

Work can provide many of these needs in various ways, although many routine and mundane jobs may cater for only a few of them. Titles and status symbols meet ideas of prestige and status. Recognition of achievement by senior management is a very important aspect of motivation.

Self-actualisation

This is the desire to fulfil one's potential. It is a desire for individual growth and creativity. It can be met in business organisations via interesting and satisfying work.

Personnel policy and human needs

Maslow's theory of human needs suggests that if a company carefully designs its jobs, it can meet the needs of most of its employees; and in so doing it can solve its motivation problem. A company could design a *personnel policy* which in outline might look as follows:

Hierarchy of Needs	Company Policy
Self-actualisation	Interesting and meaningful work. Jobs carefully designed to provide variation and interest. Job rotation. Regular training and staff development to provide people with new skills and the potential for growth.
Ego and Esteem Needs	Regular performance reviews and appraisals to set targets and to recognise achievements. Bonuses and fringe benefits linked to performance. Appropriate status symbols and titles.
Social and Belonging Needs	Careful attention paid to people's need for communication and fellowship in planning work rotas and work areas. Team work and a recognition of the importance of informal groups. Formal policies on company social events. Staff participation in company policy-making, such as works committees.
Safety and Security Needs	Company pensions and sick pay schemes. Good company safety record. Clear acceptance and compliance with the Health and Safety at Work Act, etc. Good company performance which assures permanence of employment.
Physiological Needs	Good rates of pay for the job. Staff canteen/luncheon vouchers/staff accommodation, where necessary.

For many organisations, Maslow's theory of human needs is the starting point for their personnel policy. But a company may follow a policy of the type we have outlined without it guaranteeing that all its employees are motivated. As was explained earlier, Maslow's is a universalistic theory that attempts to explain all human needs. The problem is that it does not tell us about the *particular* needs of single individuals.

A person may work for a good employer and yet be unhappy and bored with his or her job. However good an employer is, and however much thought is given to making jobs interesting and worthwhile, if people do not like what they are doing then they will feel little in the way of motivation. To understand a particular individual's motivation we need to know his or her individual feelings, hopes and fears. It is for this reason that many organisations have performance appraisal and annual review interviews in order that all employees can discuss their individual contribution to the organisation, and the organisation can look for ways of meeting their needs.

Is money a motivator?

It has been argued that people only work for money. 'Motivation', it is said, 'can be ensured by paying staff appropriately'. But money is often a poor long-term motivator, although poor rewards are considerable demotivators.

We have seen from Maslow's theory that people have complex sets of needs and, as most of us spend the majority of our lives at work, then it is work which must provide for many of our needs. Few people will work for long in a job they consider boring and uninteresting simply for the money. Some of you will say 'but many people do just that'. You may say, 'I would not do that' — pointing to another person's job — 'for all the money in the world'. Perhaps you would not, but you would need to find out what the job provides for the person doing it.

Many people do routine production line jobs because they enjoy the security of regular employment and the comradeship of the people they work with. They gain satisfaction from doing a good day's work. That is not to say that there is any particular merit in routine work, or that jobs should not be enriched and be as varied as possible. The point is that people find a variety of satisfaction in work where we might at first glance say 'they only do that for the money'.

Money is a poor motivator by itself. What is probably a better motivator is the prospect of more money. But even performance bonuses have limited effects if the work itself does not provide satisfaction. Once people are used to earning bonuses, they become a right and are taken for granted. Higher levels of bonus are then required to motivate people.

The hygiene/motivator theory

Frederick Hertzberg is an American psychologist whose contribution to the study of motivation is contained in his famous hygiene/motivator theory, which he published in his book *Work and the Nature of Man* (1966).

Hertzberg makes an important distinction between 'movement' and 'motivation'. Movement is the result of a rewards/punishment system based upon bonuses and/or the fear of sanctions. People will move — they will do things — if you threaten or bribe them, but if you want more movement you will have to threaten or bribe them again. What is more, you will have to keep upping the bribe or increasing the sanctions if people are not to return to their normal standards of work.

Motivation, by contrast, is where individuals do a good job because they want to. The nature of the work itself provides the motivation. For Hertzberg, all motivation is self-motivation.

The function of an organisation is to provide its employees with the *environment* in which they can be happy, and find methods to improve the quality of their work life. Of course, some organisations do just the opposite and provide environments which are demotivating.

Hertzberg makes a distinction between two sets of factors which affect an individual's working life. The first is *hygiene factors* — so called by analogy to physical hygiene. Hygiene prevents disease; it does not make you healthy. You have to make yourself healthy by eating properly, taking exercise, avoiding the use of abusive drugs and being careful with alcohol. What proper hygiene does is to stop you becoming unhealthy. Similarly, 'hygiene factors' do not make people happy with their jobs but they do prevent them from becoming unhappy and demotivated. Hygiene factors are environmental. They are the important things in a job which surround a worker. Among them are:

Decent pay
Decent working conditions
Good human relations — the nature of management
Company policy and administration

Hygiene factors do not motivate. Ask yourself how many 18-year-olds are motivated in their first job because the company they work for has a good pension scheme? We believe the answer is none. But many of them like to know that it is there. They like to know that their company is a good employer. It gives them confidence in the organisation.

The second set of factors is known as *motivators*. These are the things which motivate people. Motivation is the process whereby people want to do a good job and want to do it well. The motivators are:

Interesting and meaningful work
Achievement
Recognition by others of achievements
Increased responsibility
Personal growth and advancement
The opportunity to earn higher rewards

Hertzberg is clear that hygiene factors are as important as the motivators. Both sets of factors are important for the individual and the organisation.

The organisation must have its 'hygiene' right. It must provide a good environment for its employees. The company personnel policy must provide for as many needs as possible. But equally important is the requirement to provide employees with interesting and meaningful work in which they can grow and develop. People have to know that they are making a contribution to the organisation.

MOTIVATION = TRAINING + OPPORTUNITY

An important contributor to motivation is the ability to be able to do a job well. Ability is partly the result of training which provides people with the skills to do a job. Hertzberg argues that training is one of the most important ingredients in motivation. If people can do a job well, then they want to do it well. Once they have the ability, then they must be provided with the opportunity to use their ability and their talents to the full.

What should an interesting job contain?

If we follow Hertzberg's reasoning, then we ought to be able to understand what an interesting job should contain if it is one that is likely to motivate. Hertzberg is associated with the Job Enrichment Movement which seeks to enhance the interest and skill in jobs in such a way that work becomes a more interesting experience. A job should ideally be:

- A learning experience. People should be able to acquire new skills and be in a job which allows for personal growth.
- One which allows people to be responsible for checking their own work. People should not have to rely on someone else telling them whether they are doing a good job. People must be responsible for the quality of what they do.
- One that allows for direct communications. People need to talk directly to the people they need to communicate with rather than have to go through the intermediatory of a supervisor.

- One which provides people with responsibilities which are interesting and varied and which provide them with a challenge.

Activity: 'Your own motivation'

Re-read the list of factors which should ideally be present in a job. You should analyse your own job or your study in line with each heading.

   If your present occupation does not accord with each of these, ask yourself why. Would a discussion with your manager/tutor help to alter things? How could you suggest rearranging what you do to make your job study more interesting and motivating?

Equity theory

So far, by studying the theories of Hertzberg and Maslow we have been looking at what 'things' motivate people. That is to say, we have asked questions such as 'to what degree does money motivate?' or 'how do our social contacts at work affect motivation?'

What we have not discussed is how motivation takes place. Or to put it another way, the process by which individuals are motivated to do things. This is a difficult area but one which is rewarding to explore. The idea which perhaps best helps to explain the process of motivation is known as 'equity theory'. Think of it this way — people usually experience motivation if they feel that there is a proper relationship between the effort that they put into a job and the rewards which come out of it. But you may ask 'how does a person know if the rewards from a job are fair?' You may experience some glow of pride having completed a job, but it will soon disappear if you find that you receive a pat on the back while for an identical job a fellow employee has received a large bonus.

Much of our job satisfaction is based on a belief in 'equity' or 'fairness'. Fairness can be defined as 'equal work being equally rewarded'. If we find that there is not fairness in rewards then we modify our behaviour accordingly. We attempt to restore the balance of equity. If we feel that we are under-rewarded for what we do, we may restore the balance by doing less. We may reduce the quality, take a could-not-care-less attitude, or some other action which will show the signs of demotivation.

We all compare our rewards, our status, our input with those of others. It is interesting to note that our frame of reference for the comparison is with those closest to us. We may be very well rewarded compared with a starving person in a Third World country, but if we feel under-valued in our office then we will feel unfairly treated. Our comparisons are always with the situation with which we are familiar. For this reason, it is important that managers treat people in similar positions in an equal manner. There must be a degree of equity in responsibility, pay, recognition and career prospects. A certain recipe for demotivation is for some people to be seen doing all the work while others are clearly under-employed.

Activity: Equity and motivation

You should explore this idea of equity in your own role. Answer the following questions:

Do you feel that your organisation values you and the contribution that you make?
Could the organisation do more to recognise or reward your contribution?
Are you fairly treated when compared to others in similar roles?

With whom do you compare yourself in the organisation? Are those comparisons strictly fair ones? What steps have you taken to find out what other people do?

Have you ever stepped up or stepped down your performance as a result of the way you have been treated by reference to others?

Expectations and motivation

Another important element in the process of motivation is the expectation which an individual has about his or her own future. A person may be motivated to work hard at a very routine task if there is a good possibility of promotion, a bonus or some other reward at the end of it. Another individual doing the same task but with no expectations of a reward may show little sign of motivation and may only work to the required standard under pressure.

Psychologists inform us that if people are to be motivated by the expectation of rewards, then their rewards must be 'perceived' as attainable. If it is clear that by working flat out day and night there is only a small possibility of reward, then the chances are there will be no attempt at effort. Rewards must be within reach and there has to be a good track record from the organisation that individuals will receive them. Some companies deliberately build rewards into their personnel policy by *success spiralling*. They ensure at the beginning of a person's career with them that he or she achieves success. A person then builds up a favourable perception of the rewards available within the company and in consequence is motivated to achieve higher targets.

You should think about your motivation on your BTEC course in this light. If early on in your course you achieve some good grades — a Merit and a couple of Distinctions — you will probably develop expectations of these grades throughout your course. In order to meet this expectation you will probably put in extra effort. Without realising it, you are success spiralling!

An important element in expectations is your own idea of what it is you are aiming to achieve. Goal setting is very important in motivation. If there are things you are keen to achieve you will work hard to achieve them. It is more difficult to put in effort if you are uncertain about what you want in the future. Setting goals is difficult and sometimes even painful because it forces you to think about what you need to do and what you need to give up to reach them. There are exercises in this book to help in goal setting. If you find this area a difficult one, then you should spend time honestly answering them.

Job satisfaction

One of the things which most people look for in their work is job satisfaction. If you ask yourself the question 'what do I want from a job?', it is probable that one answer will be 'one that satisfies my needs'. After reading the section on Abraham Maslow this conclusion will not surprise you, but you should ponder the question 'what is it about a job that provides satisfaction?'

There are a number of aspects of work which help in the quest for job satisfaction:

Work content. The job itself must be worthwhile to the person doing it. It must be interesting and/or useful and allow a person to use his or her talents and abilities. Additionally, the content needs to be varied and the individual needs to have a degree of control over the quality of the output from the work.

Co-workers. We have already mentioned that for many people the quality of their working lives depends upon their fellow workers. People need people, and it is clear that the operation of work groups and teams plays an important part in the satisfaction people gain from their jobs. For this reason the nature of office layouts and the systems of communications, both formal and informal, play an important role.

Supervision. If you do not get on with your boss you will probably not like your job. But it is not only personal likes and dislikes which affect the nature of the supervision you receive. The consistency of management is important. If we return to the security need for a moment, it becomes clear that constant changes in policy are very unsettling. People like to know what the management's views are on issues. They like to know the rules, the boundaries of behaviour and the standards to which they must operate. Managers can assist, praise and reward behaviour — all of which are positive influences in job satisfaction.

Promotion. A career is an important aspect of job satisfaction. Most people look for opportunities for growth, development and learning in their work. They want to feel that their job is leading somewhere and that opportunities to take on other tasks and other responsibilities are available. Promotion is an important element in job satisfaction, and lack of it is a major reason for people leaving their current employment.

Pay. Money may not be a long-term motivation for many people, but it is in Hertzberg's vocabularly an important 'hygiene factor'. The money must seem right for the job. Fair pay for a fair day's work is an important element in job satisfaction.

CHAPTER 23

The Employment Process

This section will concentrate on how to apply for jobs and the measures you can take to make a success of interviews. It is written from two viewpoints. Firstly, from that of the employer looking for new recruits to the organisation and, secondly, from the standpoint of the applicant. The reason for discussing it from both angles is simply that it helps you to apply for jobs if you know what the person on the other side of the interview table is looking for.

Recruitment can be likened to a game. It is played according to a set of rules. If you do not know the rules and the tactics of the game then the chances are that the job will go to someone who does. Seeking a job is a competitive process in which some people succeed and find employment while others are disappointed.

The selection process — the employer's needs

Employers recruit people to undertake particular jobs. In return they pay salaries or wages plus certain other benefits. Employees are a source of profit to the organisation but they are also a cost. AN EMPLOYER IS LOOKING FOR EMPLOYEES WHO ARE NET ASSETS TO THE ORGANISATION — to put it simply — GOOD EMPLOYEES WILL CONTRIBUTE MORE THAN THEY COST. THEY ADD VALUE TO THE ORGANISATION.

The ideal employee will possess a long list of useful assets. Some of them will be linked to personal qualities of which cheerfulness, willingness to see a job through, efficiency and good timekeeping are examples. Employers are looking for people who present a good image to the organisation's clients and customers. Other attributes are connected with the quality of work a person can do and the way in which his or her skills can be utilised. Skills can vary enormously — fast and accurate keyboarding, ability to program in ADA, good selling skills are just a few examples. Other skills can be interpersonal, such as the way other people react to you and the way in which you relate to them.

Employers are interested in your ability to work as part of a team — will you be a loyal member of the organisation? And they will be concerned about your future potential. This last point raises questions about the person being interviewed, such as can they change and adapt as the organisation changes? Is this a person who will be able to carry additional responsibility?

Employee specification

An ideal employee may have the following attributes:

Good basic work skills — these will differ from job to job but could include a good telephone technique; selling skills; accurate keyboarding; the ability to use standard packages on a business microcomputer.
The right personal qualities for the job — these will again vary from post to post but could include the ability to work in a team; leadership skills; motivation; the ability to see a job through; respect for authority; the ability to accept responsibility.
Suitable experience, background and qualifications — these could include a relevant qualification or part-time and vacation work which could be seen as relevant to the post being applied for.
Good communications and interpersonal skills — the vast majority of jobs involve communicating with customers, clients, and co-workers. Many conflicts arise in work situations because of misunderstandings and personality clashes.
An ability to grow and develop in the job — this is difficult to measure but is of crucial importance. Employers are employing people for particular jobs but often in the certain knowledge that their needs are changing. In a fast moving business, adaptability is a key quality.

Activity: 'Describe yourself — a self-appraisal exercise'

This exercise will help you to know yourself better. You should note that there are no right answers to any of the questions below. The purpose of the activity is to give you an opportunity to evaluate yourself in a work setting.

SOCIAL SKILLS   What impact do you have on others —
How do other people react to you?
How does your appearance, manner and
speech affect others?

MOTIVATION	What is your attitude to authority?
	Do you make a good team member?
	Is leadership one of your qualities?
	What targets have you set for yourself for
	  i. next month
	  ii. next year
	  iii. the next five years?
	How do you propose to achieve these targets?
	What factors stand in the way and how will you overcome them?
	What are your expectations of your job?
	Do you always meet the targets you have set for yourself?
	Are you a person who strives for perfection in your work?
	How interested are you in your work?
	Do you have a capacity for hard work?

EMOTIONAL ADJUSTMENT	How do you cope with stress? How do you react when asked to do something you dislike? How do you react when others make critical comments about your work?
QUALIFICATIONS/ SKILLS	What skills do you possess? What qualifications do you possess? How do you intend to keep your qualifications and skills up to date?
PERSONAL	What special characteristics do you possess which make you stand out? How can you make use of your strengths of personality to achieve the things you want?

LIST YOUR STRENGTHS   LIST YOUR WEAKNESSES

In a couple of sentences describe yourself as your best friend might describe you.

Human resource planning

Before starting on the recruitment process, an employer must ask some searching questions about the people requirements of the organisation. HUMAN RESOURCE PLANNING is the somewhat awesome title given to the process, but the questions which need answering are both common-sensical and important.

- What sort of person do we need?
- How much can we afford to pay?
- How much do we need to pay?
- What sort of job is it?
- What level of skills do we need?
- Where will we get suitable candidates from?
- How much will it cost to recruit?
- What will we expect from the new person?
- Where are we going in the future and are there gaps which need to be filled in our organisation?
- What sort of people have we already in our employment?
- Are we going to employ new equipment or develop new procedures?
- Is this the time for a change?

Personnel specification

This is an option which an employer may or may not produce in writing. But all employers have at least a mental picture of the type of person they wish to employ.

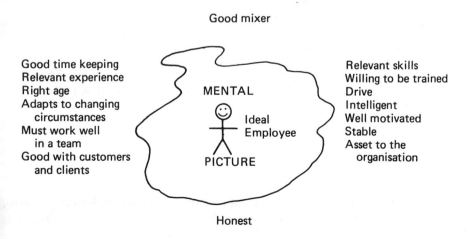

Good mixer

Good time keeping
Relevant experience
Right age
Adapts to changing
   circumstances
Must work well
   in a team
Good with customers
   and clients

MENTAL

☺ Ideal
   Employee

PICTURE

Relevant skills
Willing to be trained
Drive
Intelligent
Well motivated
Stable
Asset to the
   organisation

Honest

All organisations have their own particular requirements. It is quite easy to draw up a list of the qualities which particular organisations might require.

In Banking, a list of the following qualities may be required.

Honesty
Confidentiality
Self-discipline
Good appearance
Conventional dress sense
Good communication skills
Good interview skills
Good numeracy skills
Potential for application to detailed work

A sales assistant in a retail store might require qualities such as:

Ability to develop product knowledge
Concern for customer needs
Good oral communications
Willingness to help and to be of service
Drive and motivation
Good numeracy skills

Accounts work demands

attention to detail
good numerical skills
problem-solving skills
an ability to sit for and to pass exams

as well as a long list of desirable personal qualities.

Occupational and vocational guidance provided by the Careers Service can be very helpful if you are in any doubt about what a particular employer may be looking for.

Employee profile

Many organisations draw up an employee profile similar to this one, prior to the process of recruitment.

EMPLOYEE PROFILE			
Job title: _____			
Department: _____			
Date: _____	Essential	Desirable	Not Applicable
Physical Appearance:			
General Health Record			
Voice			
Appearance/Dress			
Build/Height			
Eyesight/Hearing			
Skills/Competencies:			
Manual dexterity			
Verbal communications			
Written communications			
Numerical skills			
Computing skills			
Job-specific skills			
Specific job training			
Keyboarding skills			
General Intelligence			
Reasoning ability			
IQ tests			
Aptitude test			
Qualifications			
Academic qualifications			
Vocational qualifications			
Training courses			
Attainments			
Previous career record			
Job experience			
Personal Disposition			
Honesty			
Motivation			
Leadership			
Team work			
Personal standards			
Ability to cope			
Adaptability/Flexibility			
Stability			
Acceptability			
Drive			
Circumstances			
Age			
Mobility			
Family circumstances			
Domicile			
Other Factors			
Driving licence			
Foreign languages			

Where do I look for a job?

Looking for a job can be a very frustrating and time-consuming activity. Like any other activity, success with job hunting can be improved by systematic planning. Part of the planning process involves being clear about the best places to find jobs. Jobs are advertised in a wide variety of places, and where to look depends on the type of vacancy you are looking for. Some of the main sources are listed below:

Careers Conventions	These are events put on by the local careers service, schools and colleges. Most of the exhibitors do not come to offer specific jobs but to talk about the opportunities in their company, industry or profession. Careers conventions are good places to meet and talk with a wide range of employers.
Newspaper Advertisements	A very important source of jobs. Local papers are one of the best places to look for local and first jobs. National advertising should not be ignored as many national schemes are advertised in the national press.
Careers Office	The Careers Service provides vocational guidance and advice about jobs, careers, education and training courses. Careers Officers regularly visit colleges.
Specialist Periodicals	Most journals carry advertisements in the areas they appeal to. *Marketing* carries posts in the fields of sales and marketing while *New Society* concentrates on social work posts. Normally these professional journals are not a good source of first jobs.
Job Centres	Department of Employment Job Centres are to be found in most High Streets and are a major source of local vacancies.
Employment Agencies and Recruitment Consultants	Private employment agencies are to be found in cities and most large towns. Many concentrate on office vacancies. They charge the firms who use their services, not the job hunter.
Vacancy Boards/Factory Gate Notices	Despite the high unemployment of recent years, a few vacancies are still advertised on vacancy boards which some companies display outside their works and offices.

Newsagents' Windows	Cards in newsagents' windows are a minor but useful source of casual and part-time work, but not a source of jobs if you are looking for a career.
Word of Mouth	A good source, provided you have the contacts. Many firms like to recruit in this way. It costs nothing and they often have a policy of employing friends and relatives of their own staff.
Commerical/Local Radio	A limited but sometimes useful source.
Your College	Many employers send vacancies directly to colleges. These can often be seen displayed on library notice boards (see figure 37).
Direct Enquiries to Companies/Organisations	A good means of finding a job. Many organisations receive a large number of direct applications about vacancies and

---

WC

WelCome Holidays Ltd
(A WelCome Group Company)

ACCOUNTANCY TRAINEE.

A keen and willing young person aged between 18 to 23 years is required by this expanding Tour Operator. The work will encompass all aspects of the accounts function with an emphasis on work with the DEC VAX minicomputer system. The post is based at the company's headquarters in Basingstoke.

Applicants should possess a BTEC National Certificate or Diploma in Business and Finance. It is expected that the successful applicant will study for the Association of Accounting Technicians qualification. A competitive salary and benefits package is offered. Letters of application giving full details of experience and qualifications should be sent by 20th January 19... to

Valerie Harcourt

Personnel Manager

WelCome Holidays Ltd
P.O. Box 26
BASINGSTOKE
HANTS.

HOLIDAYS

Figure 37   Job advertisement

training schemes and this means that they do not need to advertise vacancies. Banks and insurance companies, among other large organisations, recruit in this way. It is helpful to talk to these types of organisations to find out their requirements at a careers conference before applying.

Application forms and CVs

Employers require written details about you when you make application to them. Usually, it is on the basis of this information that they decide who they wish to interview. THE PRESENTATION OF THIS MATERIAL IS CRUCIAL IN THE PROCESS OF JOB SEARCHING.

Details about yourself can be presented in one of two ways, by

Application Form, or
Curriculum Vitae (CV)

Generally speaking, large companies with personnel departments have standard application forms. But you should not rely on having to fill one in and you are advised to prepare a CV in advance of looking for a job. Even if you do not use it, the preparation is an excellent aid for you to marshall your thoughts. It also makes you think about yourself from the employer's standpoint.

CVs

There is no one way to draw up a CV, although they do tend to follow a pattern. The best advice is to devise one that shows off your background, your skills and your potential to the full. The example in this book can be copied as a model, but you should draw up your own and go through it with someone with some experience in the field — your lecturer, an employer or someone you known who has a good record of landing the jobs they want.

Do not think of a CV as something you write once and once only. It is, as the name suggests, an account of your life and so it needs to be kept up to date and added to when significant things happen to you. Some people find it useful to keep a personal file to record details of events in their working and/or personal life. Not only does it make interesting reading from time to time but it gives you things to reflect about. When it comes to applying for jobs you have all the details you require at your fingertips. It is surprising how easy it is to forget in which month you resat an examination, went on work experience, or the address of a referee.

The best way to write a CV is to have a series of headings and then fill in the blanks. The models which follow are just that, and if you do not feel that they help you then devise your own.

The following are the usual components of a CV:

Name
Address
Telephone numbers (home and work)
Date of birth
Marital status and dependants (optional)
Present occupation or status
Employer's name and address
Previous employment history
Educational background
Qualifications
Interests/hobbies (optional)
Ambitions (optional)
Special qualities/attributes

Curriculum Vitae

Name Sheila Margaret Dudley

Address 44 Narrow Lane
Guildford
Surrey GU14 7TZ

Telephone No (0483) 783365

Date of Birth 13th May 19..

Present Occupation Full-time Student (Business Studies)
Leatherhead College of Arts and Technology

Qualifications Business & Technician Education Council
National Diploma in Business & Finance
to be completed June 19..

Units studied:
People in Organisations I & II
Organisation in its Environment I & II
Finance Keyboarding
Accounting Information Processing

Marketing   *Travel and Tourism I*
German I & II

Certificate in Pre-Vocational Education
pass June 19. .

General Certificate of Secondary Education

Subject	Grade	Date	
English Language	*A*	*June*	*19. .*
Mathematics	*D*	*November*	*19. .*
French	*B*	*June*	*19. .*
Art	*E*	*June*	*19. .*
Chemistry	*C*	*June*	*19. .*

Education

Leatherhead College of Arts and Technology
September 19. . to June 19. .

Farncombe Sixth Form College
September 19. . to June 19. .

Harold Bishop Comprehensive School
September 19. . to June 19. .

Part-Time Employment

Shop Assistant **Marks and Spencer PLC**
Leathereach Branch Saturdays and
vacations November 19. . to June 19. .

Waitress **Museum Cafe** *(Farnley)*
2 evenings a week June to October 19. .
Clerical Assistant **J. Burrows (Engineering) Ltd**
(Farnley) 6 weeks work experience March to April 19. .

Positions of Responsibility

Treasurer Leatherhead College of Arts and
Technology Students Union

Hobbies and Interests

Athletics Shot Put and Discus Throwing
3rd in County Championships 19. .

Special Attributes

Conversational knowledge of French
Working knowledge of business German
Clean driving licence

Career Ambitions

To obtain a trainee management position in a large retail
company and to progress to the position of Buyer. I
would like to travel abroad so that I can use my
languages.

Activity: 'Analysis of Sheila's CV'

Form a group with two or three other people and put yourselves in the position of the Personnel Section of a large retail group. You are analysing CVs to decide whether to call people for a job interview. You have received a CV from Sheila. The task is to analyse it and decide whether she would make a suitable trainee.

Some of the questions you should consider are listed below but they are not an exhaustive list.

- Is Sheila a competitive person? (Yours is a competitive company)
- Has she experience of retail work so that she can make an informed career choice? (You do not want someone who will leave a couple of months into the training)
- Does she indicate whether she minds moving away from home? (Your company has a policy of moving trainees around the country)
- Has she the academic background to cope with taking further qualifications?
- Are her hobbies and interests likely to conflict with her work?
- Does she show any leadership qualities?
- How much about Sheila's personality can we learn from the CV? Does she have the personality for the job?

How to write a CV

Presentation

You should always type a CV. It is your advertisement. You design it to sell yourself to a prospective employer. It should be neat, clear and legible. The easiest way of preparing one is to use a word processor so that every copy is a top copy and this makes alterations and updatings easy. This will enable you to tailor your CV to suit every application.

The employers' requirements

You should try to ensure that you provide employers with the information they want. Job advertisements will provide many of the clues. It is crucial *not* to leave important information to page 2 of your CV, as a prospective employer may not turn the page.

Headings

You should give your full name, date of birth, address and telephone number (home and work), present occupation and employer (this includes being a full-time student or a YTS trainee) on your CV. The other headings should reflect important areas of your achievements such as education, qualifications, interests and hobbies, or special attributes such as foreign languages or a driving licence.

What's next

You need to design your CV so that it shows you off in the best light. After the personal details, the order in which you list other details depends on what you think might interest an employer. If you believe that practical experience is what is being looked for, then start with details of your work experience and part-time work. If you are applying for a job which asks for certain minimum qualifications, then list your qualifications first.

Many people place their educational history after their personal details. This is not necessarily the best practice. A list of schools and colleges only tells an employer where you went and does not list your achievements. An employer will want to know what you have done.

How much detail?

The answer to this one depends on the job you are applying for, and your analysis of how much detail you need in order to sell yourself. Do not oversell yourself and try to avoid writing an autobiography. Three sides of A4 is the maximum length for a CV. You have to remember that an employer may receive hundreds of unsolicited CVs. **You must always think of the impact of your CV from the employer's angle**.

Ambitions/hobbies, etc.

The rule is to include what is relevant. You should include a few lines on your ambitions for the future, but do *not* include a vast array of hobbies and interests which will make an employer ask the question — does this person ever have the time for any work?

Special aptitudes/qualities

If you can speak French or Spanish then you should say so — and if it is only up to a conversational level then put conversational French or Spanish in the CV. A clean driving licence is very useful for many jobs and so if you possess one then you should let an employer know. A detailed knowledge of London, for example, could be very useful to a firm of London estate agents.

A covering letter

A question that many people ask is whether they should put a covering letter in with their CV. The answer, of course, depends upon the circumstances. In general, you are best advised to include a covering letter if only to say that you are sending the firm a CV in the hope that they might have a vacancy you could be considered for. You might feel that you need to add the details such as you are on holiday in mid-August and so are not available for interview. What you should not do is to repeat the information in the CV.

Do's and don'ts of writing CVs

Do's — do tell the truth
  — do have your CV typed and immaculately reproduced
  — do have a simple and conventional layout
  — do keep it factual and accurate
  — do use your date of birth but not your age (your age can date the CV)
  — do use action words where possible. Action words describe achievements and contributions, such as 'reorganised and streamlined the payroll system . . . '
Examples of action words are given below:

Completed	Created	Conducted	Funded
Directed	Eliminated	Generated	Led
Increased	Influenced	Improved	Proposed
Maintained	Managed	Restricted	Simplified
Recommended	Reorganised	Revised	
Solved	Streamlined	Strengthened	

Don'ts — don't date your CV
  — don't exceed three pages
  — don't mention salaries earned or required
  — don't mention political and religious affiliations
  — don't mention sex, race, colour or nationality
  — don't include a photograph
  — don't give reasons for leaving
  — don't have your CV written for you. Take advice such as that offered in this book, but a professionally written CV is not only

expensive but can be spotted by a Personnel Department who will wonder why you cannot draw up your own.

Application forms

Application forms vary considerably, and so the material in this section has to be general in character. Nevertheless, by following this guide you should be able to complete any firm's application form.

- Application forms should never be completed in a hurry. Speed leads to mistakes and it is better to take a photocopy of the form and then try a dry run. This will enable you to make mistakes and polish your application.
- Whenever possible type your application form. Do read the employer's instructions carefully as some employers want forms completed in hand writing. Typing an application form can be awkward and if you are going to type it have a dry run on a photocopy first. If you are going to handwrite the form use a black pen (it reproduces better on photocopiers) and make sure your handwriting is legible. **Badly written and mis-spelt forms go to the bottom of the pile.** How often have you heard people say 'I wonder why I did not get an interview for that job; it was right up my street?' — poor presentation on the application form is a major reason.
- Do not use abbreviations like BTEC, YTS, CPVE, etc. Abbreviations are a sign of laziness and not everybody understands them.
- Make certain that you include sufficient information so that an employer is clear as to what your responsibilities and duties were during any particular employment. Descriptions like 'clerk' or 'temporary office work' do not convey a great deal — they do very little to sell you to an employer.
- *Letters of application* (see figure 38). Many employers request them in conjunction with an application form. There is often space for them on the form. It is a good idea to include a letter of application (maximum length, two sides of A4 paper). The letter allows you to tell the prospective employer something about yourself. In this section there is a sample letter which Sheila Dudley, a second year BTEC National Diploma student, has written in support of her application to a retail company as a management trainee.

44 Narrow Lane
Guildford
Surrey
GU14 7TZ
Tel (0483) 783365

15 May 19.

Mrs P M Halliday
Personnel Manager
The Charlton House Group PLC
38–40 The Mount
Croydon
Surrey CR7 8UT

Dear Mrs Halliday

Application for the position of Management Trainee

I wish to add the following information to support my application for the post of Management Trainee with your company.

I am currently studying for a BTEC National Diploma in Business and Finance at Leatherhead College of Arts and Technology. I will complete the course in June of this year. The results will be published in August but as I am averaging a Merit pass on my in-course assignments I am confident of success.

The National Diploma has given me a considerable insight into how business operates, and it has provided me with a range of skills directly applicable to the work of a trainee manager. I have good written and oral skills, I can work as part of a team and I understand the financial structure of a business. In addition I can type using a range of software packages on IBM Personal System/2 computers, and I have a working knowledge of two foreign languages.

As part of my course I spent six weeks in the offices of a local engineering company. This may at first sight seem inappropriate to a career in the retail industry but in actual fact it was very useful especially as my aim is to become a buyer. The company I worked for manufactures parts for domestic electrical appliances and I had the opportunity to see how the quality control system operates. I now appreciate how important this aspect of a business is. I believe that this experience will make me a better buyer.

I have direct retail experience in a large department store as a Saturday sales assistant. From this experience I know that I have the ability to sell to customers.

I am physically fit and I am in perfect health. While I am initially interested in staying in South London I am prepared to move to another part of the country if required.

I am available for interview at any time except the first two weeks of June when I take my examinations. If you require any further information please do not hesitate to contact me.

Yours sincerely

Sheila Dudley

Figure 38   Letter of application

Activity: 'Letter of application

Read Sheila's letter of application carefully. After reading it, write a letter of application for a job which you believe will interest you. You should seek to sell yourself in the letter by concentrating on the way in which your experience and education have fitted you for the post you have in mind.

Interviews

Interviews are an important part of working life and have a number of functions. You can be interviewed for the following purposes:

Performance appraisal	Coaching
Counselling	Disciplinary matters
Exit from employment	Communication
Information gathering	Problem solving
Selection and recruitment	Promotion

Interviews will form an important part of your working life and the milestones of your career will usually be marked by one. For this reason you need to develop a good interview technique. You will be given interview practice on your course. You should make good use of it but you can also do a number of things to improve your own technique.

Preparing for an interview

An interview is a two-way process. The idea is for the interviewer to question you and for you to present yourself to the interviewer in the best possible light. The interviewer will want to see whether you will fit into the organisation or whether you are the right person to promote. Interviewees often feel at a disadvantage but remember that an interview can develop as a dialogue and that it does not have to be an interrogation. The better prepared you are, the more influence you will have on the shape and structure of the proceedings. Going into an interview room has been likened to walking into a lion's den, but you will stand a better chance if you have the rudiments of a lion tamer's skill. Remember that interviewers are human beings too and on occasions they can be as nervous as the candidates. You need to think of interviews as opportunities. They are your chance to tell a prospective employer about you or to tell your boss about your latest idea.

Appearance

Companies expect their staff to dress and to present themselves in a business-like manner. It is important that you dress smartly and appropriately for interviews. The standard of your grooming will be taken as the measure of the attention which you pay to detail. There are people who feel that work should not dictate the way they dress. The difficulty with this is that most employers hold the opposite view. The reason that firms are so concerned about standards of appearance is that their customers and clients expect a certain level of personal presentation and without it they will take their custom elsewhere. You do not have to conform in matters of dress, but you will find if you do not that your opportunities will be dramatically reduced.

Presentation

You should thoroughly prepare yourself for an interview. If it is a selection interview, you should research what the job entails and decide how you match the specifications. If it is the annual appraisal interview then you should be clear what you have achieved and what your targets are for the next year.

Our advice, based on a great deal of experience of interviewing and being interviewed, is to prepare for you performance. Too many people turn up to an interview and hope that it will go well. This is a hit and miss approach. If you decide that you want a job or a promotion, you must go all out for it.

Rehearsals

Rehearsals are the best method of preparation. You should make a list of the possible topics you could be asked about and then prepare answers to them. Ask a friend to interview you based on the questions you have prepared. Take this exercise seriously and take note of the criticisms and comments. One rehearsal is rarely enough, for you need to be certain of your style and presentation.

Rehearsals help you to reflect and they will add depth to your answers at the interview. They will put you streets ahead of the competition. If you have access to a video camera for this exercise, then so much the better as this will show you just how you look and sound and will allow you to rectify your faults.

Attitude

You need to walk into an interview room with a determination to succeed. Too many people hesitate during interviews and bring their doubts into the open. If you have real doubts or concerns at a selection interview, then the job is not for you and you are best advised to withdraw. If the doubts are minor, then the interview is not the place to air them. Sounding hesitant could lose you the job. Remember you will always have doubts about taking on anything new. You need to be clear in your own mind that the benefits outweigh the disadvantages. If that is the case, be enthusiastic at your next interview.

Selection interviews

In order to understand how best to approach a job interview, it is useful to look at the selection process from the point of view of an employer. Whether we like it or not, the prospective employer is in the position of power in the interview. But what an interviewee can do is to appreciate the employer's needs and then to prepare to meet them. In the main, employers are looking for staff who have:

- The skills to do a job well and effectively after having been given the appropriate training.
- The appropriate social and personal qualities required in the post.
- The ability to grow and to develop in the job. The successful candidate may be with the company for many years. An employer will be looking for people who can take additional responsibilities in the future, and possibly achieve promotion within the organisation.
- The ability to add value to the organisation. If the organisation is a profit-making one, then this will involve adding to the profitability of the organisation. If it is a public service organisation, then this will entail a commitment to extending the range of services available to the clients.
- A firm commitment to the aims of the organisation. Every organisation expects loyalty from its members. No organisation wants to carry passengers and the interview process often centres on the level of involvement that can be expected from a prospective employee.

Types of interview

Interviews can be structured in a number of ways, and you need to be familiar with them as a different strategy is required to deal with each of them.

Panel interviews

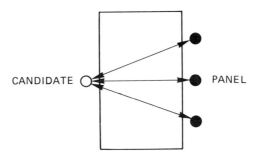

Panel interviews are common in many large organisations which have the resources to release a number of senior or middle ranking people to carry them out. Candidates for posts in local government or the Civil Service may come across them. They consist of a number of interviewers, often three, who sit across a table from the candidate. The person chairing the interview sits in the centre and usually starts off the questioning. The members of the panel each take an area of questioning — with the Chair commonly asking about background, education and previous employment. The second member perhaps probes why a candidate wants the job, while the third member will ask the technical questions to search out the candidate's suitability for the post. The person chairing the meeting may well ask additional questions and then give the candidates an opportunity to ask questions of the panel.

Face to face interviews

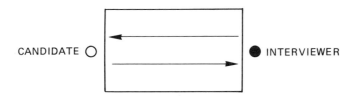

In this type of interview, it is one interviewer to one candidate. While panel interviews are almost always formal, face to face may have an element of informality about them. The table may be done away with, to remove the major barrier and to aid more informal discussion. Face to face interviews on the whole are less stressful than panel interviews, but there are certain points of difference which you need to be aware of. If you do not impress the interviewer at a face to face interview you do not have a second chance. You must try to gauge the tone, degree of formality and the attitude of the interviewer right from the start. Jokes and light hearted comments should be avoided. Jobs are responsible positions and so you cannot go wrong with a responsible attitude. You must listen carefully to questions. If you have not heard a question or are not certain of its meaning, then ask the interviewer to repeat it. It is advisable to give clear, definite answers to questions. Too many people make the mistake of assuming that a long answer is a good answer. On the other hand, yes/no answers are seldom good enough.

Rotation interviews

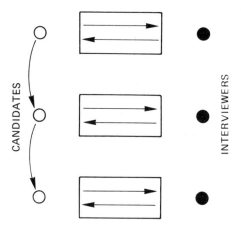

In this variation of the face to face interview, the candidate is given a number of face to face interviews with different interviewers. Usually, each interviewer asks questions on a separate topic area. Rotation interviewers give you a second chance. If you do not hit it off with the first interviewer do not despair, you may perform better at the subsequent interview.

Problem-solving sessions

These are not strictly interviews but are sometimes employed as part of the selection process as a prelude to the interview. The interviewer observes

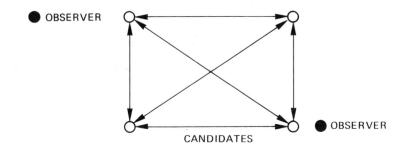

the candidates discussing a problem, solving a problem or simulating a meeting. It is an opportunity to judge candidates' problem-solving skills and their ability to deal with others.

Interview questions

As a candidate at an interview, there is little you can do to influence the questions asked of you. What you can do is to prepare for an interview and have answers for the more common questions.

Types of question

There are two main types of question.

Direct or closed questions

These are questions which prompt a YES/NO response.

> *Question* — 'Did you study French at school?'
> *Answer* — 'Yes.'

Inexperienced interviewers ask too many direct questions and consequently give candidates little chance to expand their ideas to show how they measure up to the job. If you are at an interview and are asked too many direct questions, then you need to take over and give expanded answers as follows:

> *Question* — 'Did you study French at school?'
> *Answer* — 'Yes indeed, and this year while I was on holiday in France I was able to practise my conversation. I intend to attend evening classes this year to learn business French.'

Open-ended questions

These are questions which are designed to elicit a detailed and reasoned response from the candidate. A YES/NO answer will *not* be a sufficient answer to them. They usually start with what, when, how, why, where and which.

> *Question* — 'What were your duties on the Students' Union?'
> *Answer* — 'I was the Social Secretary which involved me in organising the dances, discos and helping the various clubs and societies to hold social functions.'

You should expect *follow-up questions* from the interview panel in response to your answer from either closed or open-ended questions. You should be ready to amplify any answers you give.

Typical interview questions

The following list of typical interview questions is by no means exhaustive but is intended as a guide. If you have prepared answers to a number of likely questions, you can rehearse for the interview. You will notice that some of them are very straightforward while others require a great deal of thought and consideration. For simplicity's sake, the questions have been categorised under a number of headings.

Educational background

What qualifications did you obtain at school/college?
Where did you study?
What course did you study for at College?
Describe your course to the Panel?
What features of the course did you enjoy most?
What things did you particularly learn about business on the course?
How much of what you learnt do you think you will be able to apply in this job?
Has this course given you the ambition to undertake further study?

Family/home/locality/background

Have you lived in . . . all your life?
Do you enjoy living in . . . ?
Are any of your family employed in . . . ?
Are your parents enthusiastic about you pursuing a business career?

Are you prepared to move away from home if we posted you to . . . ?
Would you like to live and work abroad?

Ambitions/achievements to date?

Were you a school prefect at school?
Did you always want a career in business?
What are your ambitions for the future?
Where do you see yourself working in five years' time?
What is your eventual ambition?
What is it that you are looking for from a job?

The organisation

Why do you want to join this company?
What business do you think we are in?
How much do you know about us?
What do you think the job of a . . . really entails?
Why are you applying for this particular post?
How did you come to learn about us?
What can this company offer you?
What kind of position do you expect to be in four years from now?
Do you expect to spend the whole of your career with this company?

Personal qualities

What can you offer to us?
How would you describe your personality?
Would you say that you were an organised and methodical person?
What are your strengths and weaknesses?
What is it that motivates you?
Would you describe yourself as an introvert or an extrovert?
What are your hobbies and interests?

Performance Appraisal

Various names are given to the formal schemes of appraising people's performance at work including:

Staff Appraisal
Performance Appraisal/Review
Annual Review/Assessment/Interview

Many organisations have regular, formal reviews of performance sessions for all employees. In this chapter we will investigate how these are carried out, their purpose, and we will provide you with an idea of how to prepare for one. But before we start, we need to make it clear that there is a considerable debate about the advantages and the effectiveness of these systems. Some organisations, like the Civil Service, base much of their personnel policy on annual staff reviews while other organisations have no systems at all. Some writers on human relations at work have argued that a well-thought out system of appraisal is the right of every employee. While other authors have seen the process as doomed to failure because of the difficulty of exactly measuring performance in many occupations. They also highlight the practical problems of appraising people, such as the inability of many managers to tackle difficult personal confrontations which may occur during appraisal sessions.

Does every organisation have some form of staff appraisal?

The answer to this question is yes. All organisations carry out some form of appraisal. Those without formal schemes carry out informal and *ad hoc* evaluations of their employees' performance. Every time there is a promotion or a need to redeploy someone, managers have to make judgements about how well people have performed. The problem with these informal assessments is that they are usually secretive, based on insufficient information, open to bias and can be inaccurate. Most important of all is the fact that the employee is not a part of the process.

Informal assessment lacks any objective criteria or guidelines on which to judge performance. If the subordinate has a different view of what is expected from that of the manager, then assessment of performance will not be fair.

In order to overcome the shortcomings of informal assessment, a large number of organisations have instituted formal appraisal schemes.

The purpose of appraisal

Most staff appraisal schemes are based upon the annual review of performance by a person's immediate superior. Typically, it will consist of a private interview which will review the previous year's performance and set goals and targets for the following year. The arguments in favour of this process can be summarised as follows.

Staff motivation

In the chapter on motivation the point was made that the recognition of achievement is one of the most important motivators. Appraisal provides a means of providing the feedback and acknowledging achievements. It should not, of course, be the only vehicle for doing this but nevertheless there is often too little time to say 'well done', and the couple of hours set aside for the annual appraisal interview is a means of providing positive feedback (see figure 39).

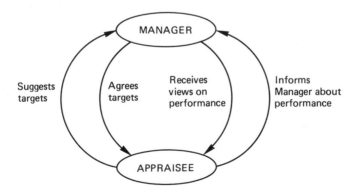

Figure 39   Appraisal provides feedback

Assessing training needs

Shortfalls in performance are often linked with inadequate training. Appraisal can assist both parties to discover training needs and to devise a training strategy to overcome problems. It may also highlight the training and development needs that are necessary if a person is to move to a more senior position.

Checking on what is happening

Managers need to know what is happening in their areas of responsibility. The appraisal interview is a means of providing this feedback. Appraisees need to check whether their actions meet the criteria managers are setting.

Rewards

Some appraisal schemes are linked to rewards and bonuses while others are deliberately separated from considerations of pay and promotion. The arguments are strong for both systems. There is a case for linking bonuses, increments and raises of salary to an employee who succeeds in meeting certain targets. The appraisal interview is the place to explore whether the targets have been met and to set the goals for next year. The opposite view says that the linking of rewards to appraisal removes some of the honesty and frankness from the process. The case is made that the purpose of the exercise is to enhance professionalism and competence, and that this element will be lost when the discussion hinges on issues related to salary.

Improving communications

Appraisal provides a forum for an employee to tell the boss what they are doing and thinking. The couple of hours set aside for the appraisal interview is a unique opportunity to talk frankly and freely. As such, it provides a valuable channel of feedback and communications.

Improving present performance

Everybody's competence can be improved. The idea of target setting is to focus on those areas requiring improved performance and specifying the standards to be achieved.

Dealing with poor or marginal performance

All organisations contain people whose performance is marginal or substandard. Organisations cannot allow that type of performance to continue but, on the other hand, a good employer must find ways of helping such employees to improve. Marginal performance cannot be left to the annual appraisal, but it does provide the opportunity for the manager and the appraisee to agree targets and the means of achieving them.

Clarifying targets and objectives

The major purpose of appraisal is to set realistic targets for employees to achieve in the next period. It is against these targets that an employee's performance will be judged the following year.

Identifying potential

Too often, talent is not recognised in organisations. Appraisal provides an opportunity to discuss ambitions, possible career moves and changes. The aim is to find and remove the barriers to the realisation of an individual's full potential.

Appraisal methods

Line or top down appraisal

This is the most common form of appraisal used by organisations. Employees are interviewed by the manager to whom they are directly accountable. It is important that the direct superior carries out the appraisal. The reason for this is that if planned organisational development is to take place, then it is the person who knows your work best with whom you should be setting and agreeing targets for the next year. That person should also evaluate how well you met last year's targets. Appraisal is based on the notion that every person is accountable to another in the organisation for the responsibilities which they have. The appraisal interview is a formal discussion of the stewardship of those responsibilities. Top down appraisal is essentially part of the management system because it:

- Confirms the lines of accountability.
- Confirms responsibilities.

- Informs both parties of priorities and objectives.
- Provides feedback on performance.
- Informs management of employees' activities.

The important element here is the skill which the manager has in conducting the interview. Such interviews need to be constructive, frank and honest. Managers need to be sympathetic and to listen, but they also need to be structured in their approach. For this reason, many organisations and/or managers use a checklist for conducting appraisal interviews. A version of this checklist is often given to employees in advance so that they know how to prepare for the interview. A sample checklist is reproduced on pages 231 and 232.

Another approach is to ask persons being appraised to set the agenda within an agreed framework. This might include a discussion of their role, details of how their job has altered in the past year, a summary of how they think they met their annual target and a list of targets for the following year.

Bottom up appraisal

Most appraisal is carried out by managers appraising their staffs. But staff are constantly appraising their bosses' performance, albeit in an informal way. Should this practice be formalised so that managers are clear on what their staff think of their management?

There are very few instances of this happening in practice, and most bottom up appraisal centres upon gossip or informal office discussion. Certain lecturers attempt this form of assessment by holding review sessions or asking their students to complete questionnaires.

The importance of the system lies in the gap which can develop in people's perception of what is occurring. A manager may see his or her role as being prudent with scarce resources, whereas the staff may regard that as being a petty and penny-pinching attitude. Again, a manager may regard office discussions as time-wasting exercises, although the staff believe them to be an important informal channel of communication.

The main reason why most organisations do not use bottom up appraisal is that managers are worried about it and its practical consequences. It is difficult to imagine formal interview situations where employees tell their boss that they think them disorganised or bureaucratic! And what sanctions do the staff have if the manager does not improve in performance?

One way around the problem is to institute some form of consultative mechanism where views can be publicly aired and at which an annual review of the organisation's work (and, by implication, the managers' leadership) can be reviewed.

Self-appraisal

From time to time you should consider undertaking an evaluation of how well you are performing at your work. You need to ask yourself questions about how well you are doing and what you are achieving. The following questions will provide a guide to the way you could start to appraise your performance.

'How often do I give time to assessing how well I am doing at my work?'

'Do I have a criterion against which to judge my performance?'

'Do I record the results of my self-analysis?'

'Do I use the results of my assessment to improve my performance?'

'What do I do if my performance does not match the criteria I have set for myself?'

Do not worry if you have never thought of undertaking this sort of exercise — most people are not this organised. But if you want to employ it, self-appraisal is a powerful tool. An awareness of self is a very important motivator and it will help to channel your energy in a positive and creative fashion.

An appraisal interview checklist

The Job
1.1 What is my current job? (List the main area of operation and responsibilities.)
1.2 What factors assist my performance in the job?
1.3 What things inhibit my performance in the job?
1.4 Does my job description need updating?

Accountability/Delegation
2.1 To whom am I accountable?
2.2 Is that accountability clear?
2.3 Am I allowed too much or too little discretion in performing my job?
2.4 Should more tasks be delegated to me? And if so, what should they be?
2.4 Should I delegate more? And if so what should I delegate and to whom?

Personal Performance
3.1 How well did I achieve last year's targets?
3.2 Why did I perform as I did?

3.3   What factors assisted my success or caused my failures?
  3.4   Were the targets I was set realistic in the light of events?
  3.5   With the advantage of hindsight could I have achieved more and done
         a better job?

Targets for the Next Period
  4.1   What targets should I expect to be setting for the next year, and why?
  4.2   What assistance will I need to achieve these targets?
  4.3   What difficulties do I see in achieving these targets?
  4.4   What long-term targets should I be setting myself?

Training and Development
  5.1   What skills do I most need to develop and why?
  5.2   What are my training needs for

         • next month
         • next year
         • the next five years?

  5.3   How can I relate these training needs to my short-term and long-term
         targets?

Personal Achievements
  6.1   What have my achievements been over the past year?
  6.2   What things in particular motivate me?
  6.3   In what situations do I do my best work?
  6.4   Why do I think I have achieved what I have?

Limitations
  7.1   What situations at work cause me the most worry and stress?
  7.2   What unsolved problems do I constantly 'take home' with me?
  7.3   What skills do I need to acquire?
  7.4   What, if any, were my failures last year and how did I attempt to
         rectify them?

Personal Effectiveness
  8.1   What impact do I make on others?
  8.2   How well do other people respond to my ideas?
  8.3   Am I listened to in discussions?
  8.4   Do I win arguments?
  8.5   Have I the ability to lead other people?
  8.6   Do I achieve the objectives which I have set for myself?

Activity: 'Preparing for the annual appraisal interview'

One of the most important parts of the appraisal process is the preparation for the interview. Ideally, both the manager and the appraisee should spend time preparing for the interview. The advantage of this is that it provides a means of self-appraisal for the appraisee, while the manager can review the level of support and assistance provided during the period. Thorough preparation will make the interview more productive and thought provoking. What follows is a list of points which should be considered by any employee before his or her annual review. Part-time students who are subject to an appraisal will find it a useful exercise to complete before their next interview, but others may also want to tackle it as a means of self-appraisal.

Prior to an appraisal interview you should:

- Produce a summary description of the work you currently undertake.
- Produce a summary of your achievements to date, stating why you consider them to have been a success.
- Produce a summary of the situations in which you feel a need to improve your effectiveness.
- Produce a summary of the problems you have been involved with and the means you have taken to tackle them.
- Produce a list of the additional skills and expertise you have developed during the year.

After you have completed this exercise you should look forward and produce:

- A series of targets for the

  next month
  next year
  next two years

- A list of the additional skills you need to develop to meet those targets.
- A list of the barriers which are currently preventing you from achieving your maximum effectiveness and the means by which you intend to overcome them.
- Details of your ambitions and the way in which you expect your career to progress.

CHAPTER 25

Opportunities and Change

History is full of examples of lost opportunities like that of the recording company who turned down the chance to record the Beatles. Individuals and companies are surrounded by potential opportunities if they have the ability to see them for what they are. You may be aware that the tank was first used by the British Naval Air Squadron because the Army could not see a military use for it, and that the Xerox copier could have been part of the IBM equipment range except that they did not have the foresight to see the huge potential market for photocopiers.

New ideas, new inventions and technologies create potential opportunities but they also threaten the stability of the world which is familiar to many people. Change is a fact of life, particularly of working life. For those of you starting your careers the one thing that we can guarantee is that the job you will finish your working life in will be nothing like the job you started in, and it will probably be a job which does not currently exist. Such is the current pace of change and technological innovation that our working lives in ten, twenty or thirty years' time will be very different from what they are today. We may speculate whether the majority of people will be engaged in full-time work as we currently know it and whether we will work from home rather than commute to offices and factories.

Whatever the reality turns out to be, the plain fact is that tomorrow's world will not be like today's. This has considerable implications for companies and individuals. Change can be a threat or an opportunity. You need to develop an attitude of mind which helps you to identify potential opportunities and develop the ability to exploit them. Companies which do not grasp at opportunities lose business, and for individuals it may mean not fulfilling their potentials.

What business am I in?

One of the most crucial questions for any business to ask is 'what business am I in?' The question is so obvious that many businesses and their senior management never ask it, and then wonder why they did not grasp an opportunity which a competitor did.

Take the example of two hotels in an expanding small town. One is the prestigious and largest hotel occupying a prime high street site. The other is smaller and has always lived in the shadow of its larger rival. Both have been approached by a company which specialises in providing fitness and dance classes. The town does not have a sports centre and Mobility Exercises Ltd are looking for an up-market venue for their activities. Both hotels have large ballrooms which are only occasionally used. The smaller hotel of the two, Bracktons, was enthusiastic about the proposal. The venture was discussed at the next Board meeting and as a result the Directors decided to undertake a thorough appraisal of their operation and their market. At the request of the Managing Director, the next meeting took the form of a brainstorming session around the idea — 'What business are we in?' Their conclusions are presented in the 'map' below.

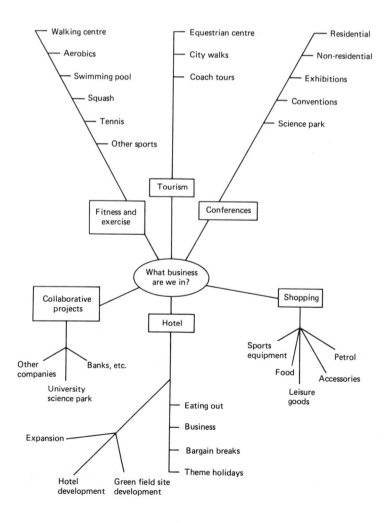

The other hotel, The Grand, took a different approach to the offer made by Mobility Exercises. Although they had plenty of space to rent, they turned the offer down. The owner, Mr Thomas, said 'We are *not* in that business'.

Two years later the Brackton Hotel changed its name to the Grange Hotel and Leisure Complex and had received planning permission to build on a green field site out of town close to the University's new Science park. The Hotel had signed a collaborative deal with Mobility Exercises and a large national hotel chain. Besides new motel facilities, the plans include a leisure complex including an Olympic size swimming pool and a nine hole golf course. In the second building phase a conference centre is planned. The local paper, *The Advertiser*, ran a front page story under the headline 'The Grange — this town's most prestigious Hotel'.

It is equally important for an individual to be aware of what business he or she is in so that opportunities can be seized and exploited when they appear. Is a person working in a bank making a career in banking or does he or she see themselves as involved in the world of finance? The latter provides greater career opportunities. Susan started work in a clerical position in the personnel department of a local authority. At her first appraisal interview her Section Leader said to her 'How do you see your career in clerical work progressing, Susan?' The Section Leader was somewhat taken aback by Susan's response which went something like this. 'Clerical work is what I currently do, but I see the opportunities being in two directions either in local government, or in personnel management in either the public or the private sector. I am currently studying for a BTEC National Certificate and that has given me the impetus to take my studies further. I see no reason why I should not reach the top in whichever field the opportunities develop'. Susan had started on the road of self-evaluation and of looking for opportunities to develop her talents. The first essential step was for her to broaden her horizon by asking the question 'What business am I going to exploit my talents in?'

Activity: 'Opportunities'

Using a map similar to that on page 235, plan out the opportunities for your future as you see it and the steps necessary to achieve your goals. You should start by putting your career goal in the centre of a blank sheet of paper and then mapping the ideas as they come to you.

The problem of change

Many people do not look for opportunities because they are not prepared to accept change. The same is true of organisations. Once they have come to terms with what they currently do, they are content to plan as though the future will resemble the present. The problem for individuals and companies who have this attitude is that the future will *not* be like the present.

Resistance to change or the lack of an opportunity-seeking philosophy leads to problems for both individuals and organisations. Markets and jobs vanish because competitors are exploiting change. This can mean that many individuals find their hard-won skills outmoded and redundant. The arrival of the computer in offices has caused considerable problems for many people in accountancy, secretarial and related occupations who have no wish to use them. But the same technology for others has enhanced their careers and provided them with new openings. New technology has meant redundancy for some and new horizons for others.

Change can be stressful and frightening, or challenging and exhilarating. The difference often stems from where you stand in relationship to those changes. If you are driving change then it can be intoxicating, but if you are a reluctant passenger then it can be depressing. Just as some people fear change, whatever the change is, so others cannot distinguish between a problem and an opportunity.

How to recognise opportunities

Opportunities are not things. In fact, for some people they seem not to exist, while for others the world is full of them. An opportunity is only there when you have seen it. But they become recognisable when you start searching for them. The important skill is to learn to seek them out and to assess the benefits which can come from them.

Opportunity seeking is a way of looking at the world but, like any other business tool, it should be used in a thorough and systematic way. It requires skills in thinking of a high order, particularly those connected with creative thought. It also connects with the skill of listening, discussed elsewhere in this book, because opportunities often arise from unexpected quarters.

SWOT

A good way of assessing new ideas is to use the SWOT analysis, which will be familiar to all of you who are studying marketing. SWOT stands for:

Strengths
Weaknesses
Opportunities
Threats

It provides you with a framework for analysing new ideas or proposals. It is sometimes the case that students after completing their BTEC course decide to set up in business for themselves. To do this they need an idea and that needs to be submitted to analysis. SWOT can help them to do this.

Andrew and Jane have decided to do just this after completing the National Diploma. The idea of being entrepreneurs appeals to them. Their first step was to decide what business to run. Jane had made money framing pictures while she was at College and that provided the germ of an idea. They decided to sell her picture-framing expertise together with antique maps, prints and the paintings of local artists. They knew they could not afford premises, but Jane's father offered them his garage and they decided to hire stalls in different towns on market days and to attend antiques fairs which are usually held on weekends. Andrew and Jane know they will need to put together a detailed business plan for submission to their bank manager in order to obtain a start up loan, but before they do this they have undertaken a SWOT analysis to see how their idea stands up to scrutiny.

Picture-framing business — SWOT analysis

Strengths	Weaknesses
1. Resolve to make a success of the venture	1. No business experience (except part-time and work experience)
2. Skills in picture framing and some track record of success (Jane)	2. Where does the business lead us?
3. Basic Business knowledge gained on National Diploma course	3. The idea is appealing, but there are others in the same business and the market has only limited elasticity
4. Backing of parents	
5. Initial market survey shows the idea has promise	4. Loss of time when we could be establishing ourselves in a career
6. Idea requires little capital and so the only risk is loss of time and salary opportunities foregone	5. We do not know whether we will make money
7. Enthusiasm, drive and ambition	
8. Good selling skills (Andrew)	

Opportunities	*Threats*
1. Business idea has the potential to be diversified into many areas: antiques, home interiors, design, etc.	1. There is competition from retail outlets who could temporarily reduce prices to drive us out of business
2. Will develop essential entrepreneurial skills and experience which can only be developed through practice	2. The cost of the start up loan
3. Potential for a good return on modest initial outlay which can help the build up of expansion capital	3. Difficulty of breaking into an already established market
4. Helps to establish a network of contacts for other entrepreneurial opportunities which might develop	4. Do we need planning permission to run the picture framing side of the business from Jane's father's garage?
	5. Will a bank lend us the money to start up?

Activity: 'New ideas'

Working in a group, develop a number of ideas for entrepreneurial ventures which you should submit to SWOT analysis.

Career planning

Careful career planning is a good example of looking for opportunities and taking advantage of them when they arise. It helps to be in the right place at the right time, but it is also possible 'to make your own luck' so that you are ready to take advantage of an opportunity when it arises.

Careers do not just happen: except for the lucky few, the rest of us have to work hard to plan and make our own careers.

Assuming you want a career, what can you do to make it happen? Firstly, you need to start with a self-evaluation of yourself, your current performance in your job or course of study and to analyse them in relation to the career you have in mind. You need to ask yourself whether you enjoy what you are currently doing and whether you will continue to enjoy it in the future. This is a difficult question to answer, but it is important because enjoying a job is a major source of motivation as well as personal satisfaction.

Do you have the qualities that are required for your chosen career? To answer the question you need to build up a knowledge of the skills and experience required. Do you possess them? Do you know what they are? If you do not, then you will need to go about finding out what you will require.

Are you prepared to do the things that are necessary to make a success of your chosen career? This may involve moving home, undertaking years of study, learning a foreign language, working long and unsociable hours, acquiring skills and gaining competencies in new areas. You must ask yourself whether you have the dedication, motivation and the desire to succeed. Only you know how single minded you can be.

Are you reading the necessary journals, magazines and newspapers to keep abreast of developments in your chosen field? The relevant press will carry job advertisements which will provide you with an idea of what you can aim at and the type of post you can expect to fill at particular ages and stages in your career. You must know your chosen field and reading the technical press is an invaluable aid.

You must set yourself long-term AIMS, and shorter-term GOALS. Your aim might be to set up on your own in the retail business. Your goals in this instance should be to become a departmental manager in a large retail chain by the time you are twenty-five in order to acquire the necessary background in retail management.

Once you have established the aims and goals, then you need a STRATEGY. How are you going to achieve what you have set yourself? Your strategy might be to apply for a place on a management traineeship scheme with a number of retail chains. If you are a full-time student, you might find weekend or vacation employment in a retail store to make certain that the career is what you think it is.

You need to draw up a CV and then keep it up to date.

You should periodically review your career. This will involve asking yourself how well you are doing in achieving your short-term goals. You should consider whether the path you have decided to travel is still the right one for you, or whether your experience has opened up new vistas for you. Do not be afraid to think of new directions but do evaluate them as carefully as you did your original intentions.

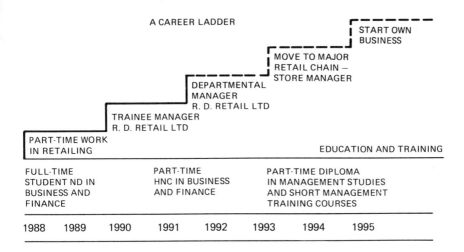

A CAREER LADDER

START OWN BUSINESS

MOVE TO MAJOR RETAIL CHAIN — STORE MANAGER

DEPARTMENTAL MANAGER R. D. RETAIL LTD

TRAINEE MANAGER R. D. RETAIL LTD

PART-TIME WORK IN RETAILING

EDUCATION AND TRAINING

FULL-TIME STUDENT ND IN BUSINESS AND FINANCE

PART-TIME HNC IN BUSINESS AND FINANCE

PART-TIME DIPLOMA IN MANAGEMENT STUDIES AND SHORT MANAGEMENT TRAINING COURSES

1988   1989   1990   1991   1992   1993   1994   1995

A *career planning map*

There are a number of ways to evaluate your career progress. Some people like to think in pictures, and they find that drawing up the kind of chart which follows helps them to clarify their thinking. In this example, both actual and expected career developments have been mapped as have educational and training experiences.

Activity: 'Career planning'

In relation to your own career aspirations list:
Your long term AIMS
Your intermediate career GOALS
The STRATEGIES you intend to employ in order to fulfil your aims.
Draw a map of your intended career progression

SECTION V

ASSIGNMENTS

① Mapping the College's Structure

1 *General Objectives*
   A Understand the principal features of organisational structures and operations and how these affect the communication system of an organisation.
   B Give and exchange information.
   E Present and disseminate information, using appropriate means.
   G Recognise factors which contribute to efficient working within an organisation and ways this can be assessed and influenced.

2

Indicative content	Skills
Levels of responsibility and authority in specific organisations.	Working with others.
	Communicating.
	Information gathering.
Support-systems—administrative, technical and clerical.	Information processing.
Oral and written information.	
Presentation of organisation charts and communication in diagrammatic form.	
Identification of levels of responsibility and authority	

3 *Links with other Units*
   Organisation in its Environment.
   General Objectives A, B, D, E.

4 *Introduction*
This Assignment is designed so that you can research the way in which an organisation operates. The organisation chosen is one with which you are all familiar — the College. This Assignment is designed both for group and individual activity.

5 *Activities*
5.1 Collect as much of the official information that you can about the College. This will include full and part-time prospectuses, student union handbooks, a sample of course leaflets, information for visitors, etc.

5.2 From the information you have collected, rough out an organisation chart of the College showing its main divisions and activities. This will give you a guide for the hard work which comes next.

5.3 Each group should select an area of the College's work to research. In order to do this you should:

- Invite a senior member of the College — Principal, Vice-Principal, Head of Department — to talk to you about the structure and goals of the organisation.

- Draw up a questionnaire on which to base your research. The purpose of this is to give your research direction. You will want to know about:
  — the goals of the area of the College you are researching.
  — the number of staff and students working in it.
  — the courses that are offered.
  — the formal reporting mechanisms.
  — the means by which it links with the wider community of parents, employers and schools.
  — the future plans of the college.
  — the formal structure of relationships.
  — the communication methods and structure.

5.4 Your next task is to write a report on your research paying particular attention to the policy goals, the communications system and the main structure of relationships. You should include an organisation chart in the report.

5.5 Each group should make an oral presentation of its main findings to the rest of the class and you should organise a forum so that you can debate the similarities and differences between the various aspects of the College which have been researched.

5.6 Each individual should produce a written report on the structure of the College, paying particular attention to the differences between the areas he or she researched and those researched by other groups.

② The Press Release

1. *General Objectives*
   B   Give and exchange information.
   C   Examine information systems and their impact on an organisa-
       tion's operations, in terms of the use of a range of formats for
       information handling.
   E   Present and disseminate information, using appropriate means.
   F   Appreciate the importance of personal relationships and the social
       environment.

2

Indicative content	Skills
Oral and written communications.	Communicating
Organisation's external methods of communications.	Information processing.
Relevance of format to content, purpose and intended recipient.	Identifying and tackling problems.
Design, structure and use of appropriate formats for a variety of uses.	
Adaptation of messages to the needs of different recipients.	

3   *Links with other Units*
    Finance.
    General Objective B.

    Organisation in its Environment.
    General Objective B.

4   *Introduction*
    The purpose of this activity is to give you the opportunity to learn how
    to write a press release to be sent to a local newspaper.

5   *Role*
    You are employed in the Press and Public Relations Department of
    your local district council. Your boss has had a request from the Leisure
    Services Officer to write a piece on the new Bowling Club in Central
    Park. To help you, the Leisure Services Officer has sent you a copy of
    the relevant Council Minutes.

6

Council Meeting
14th December 19..

Report of the Leisure Service Committee
_____

Central Park Bowling Club

At the last meeting the Council approved the principle of financial assistance to the Central Park Bowling Club on land leased to the Club by the Council. Terms have now been provisionally agreed with the Club for the surrender of the existing lease and the grant of a new lease. The existing lease will expire on 31st January 2009 and will be surrendered probably on the 21st January next year, and a new lease granted to the club.

The Leisure Services Committee RECOMMEND:

a) The surrender of the present lease and the grant of a new lease to Central Park Bowling Club.
b) The lessees to erect at their expense a four rink indoor club, with a wide range of social and recreational facilities, including bar, cafeteria, snooker and lounge areas.
c) That the lessees will allow the general public areas at reasonable rates at agreed off peak times.

The lease includes 3,332 square yards of land on the area coloured pink on the attached Map.

---

7   The Leisure Services Officer has attached the following memo:

TO: Press and Public Relations Office
FROM: Leisure Service Office.   21st May 19..
SUBJECT: Press Release — Bowling Club
          _____

I am anxious that a story about the new Central Park Bowling Club appears in next week's press. The attached Council Minutes gives all the facts. I think that to save time you could just send the newspaper a copy of the minutes.

                                                          L.D. Reed
                                                  Leisure Service Officer

---

8   Do you agree with Mrs Reed? Does the Council Minute provide the kind of riveting material that a busy editor at the local paper will want to read and then will have to rewrite?

There is nothing wrong with the style of the Council Minute. It is perfectly adequate for its function as a record of Council decisions. But people read local newspapers for interest and entertainment and so this story must be told in a different way for that audience.

9   *Task*

Your task is to turn this Council Minute into a Press Release which with only limited editing could be published as a newspaper article. To help, read through some typical local stories in your own press and absorb some of the flavour of their style. To help you to do it here are some guides:

Think in pictures. Try to visualise the facilities being provided by the Council and the type of people who might use them. What type of people would be interested in the story — visualise them.
Write as you speak. Write in a clear and rhythmical way. Imagine when you are writing that you are telling someone a story.
Picture a typical interested newspaper reader and write for them.
Find a good headline. This will help you start to write. As you sit in your office, the other Press Officer comes across to your desk and you show her the minutes. She suggests some possible headlines.

'OAPs bowled over by Council decision'.
'Council agrees public can bowl in'.

Start with the most important thing you have to say. This will grab the readers' attention and make them want to read on. Start with your theme or conclusion and then present your evidence or the detail to back it up. Technically, this form of presentation is known as the INVERTED PYRAMID. It is a good way to write for a newspaper because if the Press Release is too long for the space available, then editors tend to cut off the last paragraph or two. If you have put your important information first and the least important material last, then action of this kind will not spoil your story.

Your press release should be about 300–400 words in length. The important point to remember is that it must be lively and readable.

③ Applying for a job

1 *General Objectives*
   B Give and exchange information.
   C Examine information systems and their impact on the organisa-
      tion's operation.
   D Assess the uses of electronic technology as a means of communica-
      tion.
   F Appreciate the importance of personal relationships and the social
      environment.

2

Indicative content	Skills
Social skills in the work context.	Communicating.
Interviewing skills.	Working with others.
Effective presentation.	Information gathering.
Verbal and non-verbal communication.	Information processing.
Application of basic word processing packages.	Design and visual discrimination.
Developments of materials relating to job advertisements, etc.	

---

3   *Links with other Units*
    Organisation in its Environment
    General Objectives B, L, M.

    Finance
    General Objective F.

4   *Introduction*
During this assignment you will be following the process which you have to take when applying for a job. These activities will give you personal experience of job searching skills, and they will also allow you to simulate the process which employers undertake when they recruit and select employees.

5   *Activities*
5.1   You should start by reading the section in chapter 23 on places to look for a job. Decide on a career area which interests you — such as banking, insurance, travel, sales — and then collect advertisements for posts in that area which you might apply for once you have completed the course.
5.2   In small groups of, say, three or four, consider the advertisements which you have all collected. You should then decide on what organisation your group is to be and then advertise for a new employee who has recently completed a BTEC National Course in Business and Finance. You will have to decide on the type of organisation you are working for and the type of products/services

you are involved with. Your studies for the Organisation in its Environment unit will assist here.

You should then:

- Design a suitable advertisement.
- Draw up a list of appropriate places to advertise. In addition you must calculate the costs of your advertisement. (Your college administration will have details of the cost of advertisements in national and local papers. You should write a memorandum to the Chief Administrative Officer requesting this information.)

5.3   Once you have designed the advertisement you should:

- Draw up a job description for the post.
- Prepare a personnel specification. (You should put this information on a word processor so that copies are available for the interview panel.)
- Decide on how you are going to interview for the job. You should then prepare for the interview and list the questions you are going to ask. (You should read the information in Chapter 23 on types of interview so that you can use a suitable format.)

5.4   Once you have completed activities 5.1–5.3, you should pass your advertisement to another group and they will then pass you theirs. You should now work individually to prepare for your own interview. You will be interviewed by members of another group. In order to prepare for your interview you should:

- Write a suitable letter of application.
- Write a CV.

5.5   You will now need to prepare for your own interview. As we said in the section on interviewing in chapter 23, it is important for you to rehearse properly as part of your interview preparation.

5.6   You are required in your groups to form a selection panel and to interview the members of another group for the post in your organisation. You should arrange for one member of your group to operate a video camera so that you have a visual record of the interviews. You can take it in turns to carry out this exercise.

At the end of each interview make a brief report on each candidate.

5.7   Arrange a feedback session so that both interviewers and interviewees can see and discuss their performance.

5.8   In order to make the task more realistic, you should arrange for local employer(s) to come to the college and to hold a mock interview with your group. You could approach a person from the firm where you did your work experience to carry out the exercise. You could ask the employer to draw up the job specification for the interviews or else provide the ones which you have produced for this assignment.

④ **Facing up to Change**

1 *General Objectives*
   F   Appreciate the importance of personal relationships and the social environment.
   G   Recognise factors which contribute to efficient working within an organisation and ways in which it can be assessed and influenced.
   H   Assess the relationship between the working environment and an employee's performance.
   I   Identify the constraints and the opportunities of group working, sources of conflict and methods of conflict management.
   J   Analyse changes which affect the work of individuals and groups within organisations.

2

Indicative content	Skills
Social skills in the Work Context.	Communicating.
Flexible response to Personal factors.	Interpersonal skills.
Effective presentation of ideas.	Presenting information.
Management styles in different situations.	Working with others.
Job enrichment and job satisfaction.	
Needs of people at work.	
Skills and attitudes associated with new working methods.	
Reorganisation of work and systems.	

3 *Links with other Units*
   Organisation in its Environment
   General Objectives D, E, F, G.

4   *Introduction*
    This activity is designed to assist you to think about the ways in which
    technological change should be handled.

5   *Scenario*
    George Barker and Partners Ltd is an expanding building and civil
    engineering company with a design and drawing-office section. The
    section is supported by four women, two designated as Secretaries and
    two others whose job titles are Secretarial Assistant. The Secretarial
    Assistants do a considerable amount of copy-typing in their work. The
    Secretaries do a wide variety of jobs mainly in a Personal Assistant
    capacity to the leading designers. Their work is very responsible and a
    considerable amount of it involves client liaison and organising meet-
    ings. The section works efficiently and the staff are happy and
    contented with their jobs.

    The new Managing Director, Frank Barker, is keen to update work
    practices in the company. One day four personal computers, complete
    with word processing and database software, arrive in the office. The
    following memorandum was sent to the Secretarial staff.

To: Secretarial Support Section
From: M.D.
Subject: Personal Computers

You will be delighted to see that we are now up-to-date at last. I am assured that the
equipment is user friendly and training has been arranged for Monday and Tuesday
next week on our premises. I am arranging for the old typewriters to be removed on
the Thursday.

Good Luck with this new venture. It will, I am sure, be an interesting experience.

On the morning before the training was due to begin, one Secretary
and one Secretarial Assistant had given in their notice. The other two
had requested to see the Managing Director, and he had heard it
rumoured that they are going to refuse to use the new machines.

6   *Your role*
    Frank Barker needs to salvage the situation. He is travelling abroad
    tonight for an important meeting. You are the newly appointed
    Technical Services Assistant Supervisor and although the Secretarial
    Support Services are not your direct responsibility, he has asked you to
    solve the problem and overcome the women's resistance to change.

7 *Activity*

- Analyse the problem, paying particular attention to the communications and human relation aspect of the situation.
- What would you have done if you had been in charge of the project
  from the beginning.
- Write a report to the Managing Director. In it you should say what
  measures you have taken to remedy the problem. In a diplomatic
  manner, outline to him the problem as the secretarial staff see it.
- As a result of your report, the Managing Director has asked you to
  carry out a full Organisation and Methods study of this area of work
  with a view to updating procedures and equipment. He requires a
  memorandum stating how you would intend to carry out the
  project.

⑤ Systems Analysis

1 *General Objectives*
   A   Understand the principal features of organisational structures.
   C   Examine information systems and their impact on an organisation's
       operations, in terms of the use of a range of formats for informa-
       tion handling.
   D   Assess the uses of electronic technology as a means of communica-
       tion.
   E   Present and disseminate information, using appropriate means.
   G   Recognise factors which contribute to efficient workings within an
       organisation, and ways in which this can be assessed and
       influenced.
   H   Assess the relationship between the working environment and the
       employee's performance.

2

Indicative content	Skills
Information storage.	Information gathering.
Support systems.	Information processing
Design, structure and use of	Identifying and tackling
appropriate formats for a	problems.
variety of uses.	Communicating.
Reports for specific purposes.	
Impact of computers.	
Use of basic documentation	
systems and procedures.	
Diagrammatic representation	
of business information ways	
of assessing efficiency in	
organisations, for example,	
systems analysis.	
Organisation and Methods.	

3 *Links with other Units*
   Organisation in its Environment
   General Objectives B, E, F, K, M

4 *Introduction*
   This assignment places you in the role of a systems analyst who is looking critically at the efficiency of a system. It will involve you in researching a system either in your own organisation (if you are a part-time student) or in an organisation where you are doing work experience (full-time student). You will be required to produce a written report of your findings for the senior management of the organisation.

5 *Activities*
5.1 Select a system for critical evaluation. It can be a paperwork or a computerised system, but it should preferably be one with which you are familiar. It would make sense to choose a system in consultation with your immediate superior/manager. There may be a system ripe for investigation.
5.2 Your investigation should include the following:

   • A detailed description of the workings of the present system including its objectives and outcomes.
   • A flowchart of the process.

- Notes on its strengths and weaknesses.
- An examination of whether or not the system meets the objectives set for it. (In order to do this, you will need to ask questions of the people concerned with administering the system and you should design a questionnaire/checklist to make certain that you ask the right questions and have a means of cataloguing the replies.)
- Propose ways in which the system can be redesigned to improve its effectiveness.
- Flowchart the proposed system.
- Produce reasoned recommendations for your new system.
- Describe any changes to the structure of the organisation which may be required as a result of the change.
- Comment upon the human problems which may be involved in your proposed systems change.

Bibliography

Study

Sandra Ashman and Alan George, *Study and Learn*, Heinemann, 1982.
Robert Barrass, *Study!*, Chapman and Hall, 1984.
Edward de Bono, *Six Thinking Hats*, Viking, 1985.
Tony Buzan, *Use Your Head*, Ariel Books/BBC, 1982.
Sally Garratt, *Manage your Time*, Fontana, 1985.

Communication

K. E. B. Bakewell, *How to Organise Information*, Gower, 1984.
Peter Clark, *Using Statistics in Business 1 and 2*, Pan, 1982.
Richard Dimbleby and Graeme Burton, *More Than Words*, Methuen, 1985.
Desmond W. Evans, *People, Communication and Organisation*, Pitman, 1986.
Stewart Marshall and Noel Williams, *Exercise in Teaching Communications*, Kogan Page, 1986.
Casey Miller and Kate Swift, *The Handbook of Non-sexist Writing for Writers, Editors and Speakers*, The Women's Press, 1985.
Nick Moore and Martin Hesp, *The Basics of Writing Reports Etcetera*, Clive Bingley, 1985.
C. J. Parsons and S. J. Hughes, *Written Communications for Business Studies, 3rd edition*, Edward Arnold, 1981.
Nicki Stanton, *What Do You Mean 'Communication'?*, Pan, 1982.
L. A. Woolcott and W. R. Unwin, *Master Business Communication*, Macmillan, 1983.

Organisations and Information Systems

R. Bearman, *Small Business Computers for First Time Users*, NCC Publications, 1983.

Robin Bradbeer, *Choosing a Business Microcomputer*, Gower, 1982.

Wilfred Brown, *Explorations in Management*, Penguin, 1965.

David A. Buchanan and Andrzej A. Huczywski, *Organisational & Behaviour — an Introductory Text*, Prentice-Hall International, 1985.

Charles Hardy, *Understanding Organisations*, Penguin, 1976.

Elliot Jacques, *A General Theory of Bureaucracy*, Halstead Heinemann, 1976.

Charles Jones, *The Computer Handbook. A Businessman's Guide to Choosing a Computer System*, Macmillan, 1986.

Andrew Leigh, *Understanding Management Software*, Macmillan, 1986.

Douglas McGregor, *The Human Side of Enterprise*, McGraw-Hill, 1960.

W. David Rees, *The Skills of Management*, Croom Helm, 1984.

George Thomason, *Job Evaluation Objectives and Methods*, Institute of Personnel Management, 1980.

Emile Woolf, Suresh Tanna and Karam Singh, *Systems Analysis and Design*, Macdonald and Evans, 1986.

Mike Smith *et al.*, *Introducing Organisation Behaviour*, Macmillan, 1982.

Peter Zorkoczy, *Information Technology — An Introduction, 2nd edition*, Pitman, 1985.

People

Michael Argyle, *The Psychology of Interpersonal Behaviour*, Penguin, 1985.

Derek Biddle and Robin Everden, *Human Aspects of Management*, Institute of Personnel Management, 1980.

R. L. Boot, A. F. Cowling and M. J. K. Stanworth, *Behavioural Science for Managers*, Edward Arnold, 1982.

Cary L. Cooper and Peter Makin, *Psychology for Managers*, Macmillan, 1984.

John Munro Frazer, *Employment Interviewing*, Macdonald & Evans, 1978.

Judy Gahagan, *Interpersonal and Group Behaviour*, Methuen, 1978.

Frank G. Goble, *The Third Force. The Psychology of Abraham Maslow*, Pocket Books, 1970.

Frederick Hertzberg, *Work and the Nature of Man*, World Publishing, 1966.

Gerry Randell, Peter Packard and John Slater, *Staff Appraisal*, Institute of Personnel Management, 1975.

W. J. H. Sprott, *Human Groups*, Penguin, 1958.

Ian Winfield, *Human Resources and Computing*, Heinemann, 1986.

Index

Accent 31–2
Accountability 116–17
Advertisement, for jobs 209
Application forms 210, 216
Appraisal *see* Performance appraisal
   and Personal appraisal
Arguments, structure of 185–6
Assertiveness 185–6
Assignments 5–7
Authority 118–19

Bar charts 69–71, 75
Brainstorming 14–15
Brown, Wilfred 111
Bubble charts 77
Bureaucracy 119–20
Burns and Stalker 111
Business Names Act 1985 38

Career planning 239–41
Central processing unit 88
Change 147, 234–41
Colleges of further education 117–18
Communications
  barriers to and breakdowns 27–9
  by computer 93–4
  definition of 26–8
  oral 29–30
  persuasion 185–9
  putting a message across 182–3
Companies Act 1985 39
Computers
  and change 145–6
  communicating by 93–4
  hardware and equipment 86–9
  history of 84–5
  language of 85–6
  networking 94–7
  software 89–93
  voice recognition 85

Confidentiality, in letter writing 45–6
Contingency theory 124
Corporate identity 37–8
Corporate plan 148
Creativity 12–16
Curriculum vitae 210–16

Data Protection Act 1984 91
Databases 90–1
Delegation 120–1
Demand curve 72, 74
Desk top publishing 67
Dialects 31–2
Diaries and learning 8, 18–19
Discriminatory language *see*
   Non-discriminatory language
Disk drives 88

Employment
  application forms and CVs 210–16
  career planning 239–41
  employee profile 206–7
  employee specification 203–4
  interviews 218–25
  job search 208–10
  letters of application 216–18
  selection process 202–3
Equity theory 198–9
Expectations and motivation *see*
   Motivation

Filing systems 140–3
Formal structures 112–15

Gate keepers 183
Glazier Metals 111
Goals 3–5
Graphs 72–5

Groups
  behaviour 172
  effectiveness 172–3
  formal and informal 169–70
  formation 171
  interactions 176–7
  roles of 174–5
  stages of development 171–2

Handy, Charles 125
Hardware, computer 86–9
Hertzberg, Frederick 196–7
Hidden agenda 134–5
Hierarchies 120–2
Hierarchies of needs *see* Motivation
Human resource planning 204–5
Hygiene factors *see* Motivation

Informal structures of
    organisation 112–15
Information
  sources 143–5
  systems 138–46
  technology 112–15
Interviews
  appraisal 231–3
  selection 218–25

Jacques, Elliot 111
Job
  advertisements 209
  enrichment 197–8
  satisfaction 200–1
  search 208–9
Job evaluation
  analytical methods 159–60
  job ranking 158
  paired comparisons 159
  points ratings 161–2

Keyboarding 85
Keywords 15–16

Language
  and change 99
  non-sexist *see* Non-discriminatory
    language
  of computers 85–6
  racism in language *see*
    Non-discriminatory language
Leadership 123–4
Learning 3, 12
Letters
  functions 36–7

layout and style 39–45
  letterheads 37
  standard paragraphs 49
  statutory requirements 38–9
  tone and style 48–9
Listening 28, 33–5
Logos 37–9

Management
  by objectives 147–8
  style 123–5
  time management 6–7, 17–21
Managers 101, 122–3
Maslow, Abraham 192
Matrix structures 109–10
McGregor, Douglas 123
Mechanistic organisations 110–11
Meetings 130–7
Memorandum
  format 51–2
  style of 53–4
  use of 53
Minutes of meetings 136
Money, as a motivator 195, 201
Motivation 33–4, 190–201
  and equity theory 198–9
  and expectations 199–200
  and hierarchy of needs 192–4
  and hygiene factors 196
Mouse, computer input device 87

Needs *see* Motivation
Networking computers 94–7
Non-discriminatory language 98–101,
    132
Norms, of groups 170
Note-taking 7–10

Opportunities 234–41
Organic structures 110–11
Organisation and methods 149–53
Organisations
  and technological change 110–11
  design of 107–10
  formal and informal
    structures 112–15
  mechanistic structures 110–11
  organic structures 110–11
  structure of 107–10

Performance appraisal 226–33
Personal appraisal 231
Personal contacts 184–5
Personal identity 181–2

Personnel policy and human
  needs   193–5
Personnel specification   205–6
Persuasion   186–9
Pictograms   78–9
Pie charts   68, 75–7
Power   125–6
Presentation   *see* Self-presentation
Press releases   64–6
Punctuations, open and close style for
  letters   40–3

Quality circles   177–8
QWERTY keyboard   85, 87

Rational behaviour   191
Reports
  visual presentation of
    information   67–8
  writing   60–3
Roles   181–2

Salary differentials   154–5
Self-presentation   180–9
Sexist language   *see*
  Non-discriminatory language
Slang   32–3
Software   89–90
Span of control   127
Speech   31–3
Spreadsheets   89–90
Staff and line   127–8

Staff appraisal   *see* Performance
  appraisal
Status   128–9
Stereotyping   181
Study   3–11, 17–21
Supply curve   74
SWOT   237–9
Synergy   167
Systems analysis   149

Talks
  preparing for a talk   80–2
  to an audience   81
  use of visual aids   82
Telephone
  making calls   58–9
  receiving calls   58–9
Theory X and Y   123–4
Thinking   12–15
  critical and creative   13–14
  lateral   15
Time, managing time   6–7, 17–21

Videotex services   144–5
Visual aids   82

Word processing   91–3
Work group   *see* Groups
Work study, work
  measurement   151–2
WYSIWYG   87